HOLD ON TO YOURSELF

How To Stay Cool in Hot Conversations

JUDY ZEHR,
COUPLE AND FAMILY THERAPIST

AND

JULIA MENARD,
ORGANIZATIONAL CONFLICT MEDIATOR

BALBOA
PRESS
A DIVISION OF HAY HOUSE

Balboa Press books may be ordered through booksellers or by contacting:

Balboa Press
A Division of Hay House
1663 Liberty Drive
Bloomington, IN 47403
www.balboapress.com
1 (877) 407-4847

Print information available on the last page.

ISBN: 978-1-5043-5106-5 (sc)
ISBN: 978-1-5043-5107-2 (e)

Balboa Press rev. date: 08/16/2016

If you are directly involved in a conflict, or working in the middle of one as a mediator, this book is going to help you stay cool and communicate effectively. Julia Menard and Judy Zehr's practical tools based on insights from the field of neuroscience and years of experience are refreshing when many of us have begun to think that there is not much new under the sun of communication.

--**Dr. Ben Hoffman**, author of *Peaceweaving: Shamanistic Insights into Mediating the Transformation of Power*

Judy Zehr and Julie Menard present a powerful array of ideas and skills based in neuroscience to navigate the most difficult and challenging interactions. Their ease of style and accessible tools make this book a go-to for learning conflict prevention and resolution.

--**Connie Henderson,** LCSW Therapist and author, Mammoth Lakes, CA

It's impossible to avoid conflict, and if we want to get better at it we need to train our minds! In this incredibly practical new book, Julia Menard and Judy Zehr give us the tools to do just that. Blending the best of neuroscience with the latest tools and techniques, they help us understand what's really going on in our brains when we get into conflict - and what we can do about it! As a coach I love the accessible tools, conflict myths, refreshing new beliefs about conflict and the mindfulness practices. These are invaluable in helping my clients improve their relationships and master the skill of having difficult conversations.

--**Emma-Louise Elsey,** professional life coach and Founder of The Coaching Tools Company

As a social worker and life coach, I have supported many individuals and groups to cope with high stress, trauma and burnout through helping them to access and create the inner state of calm that fosters balance and well-being while standing in the heat. The title of this book by Judy and Julia says it all "Hold On To Yourself" – as it is the key to supporting both yourself and others during times of conflict and stress. This book is filled with the art, heart and science of how to thrive during times of stress and conflict. In it you will learn the "5 Practices to Strengthen the Vagal Brake" – put this brake on and you are sure to thrive when the heat is on. And you will help others do the same. This book helps you create a win-win during conflict and beyond.

--**Lynda Monk**, MSW, RSW, CPCC, Writing for Wellness Coach, Speaker, Bestselling Author & Founder of Creative Wellness

Judy Zehr and Julia Menard have joined forces to create this compassionate and clearly written self-help tour de force. Even readers already familiar with the topics of stress, neuroscience, and communication skills will find new information to help them recognize and deal better with the kinds of challenging interactions we all experience in the various contexts of our lives. Original thinkers and experts in communication in their own right, the authors draw comfortably and seamlessly from a variety of theoretical and practical approaches, resulting in an excellent compendium of easy-to-use, yet powerful tools.

--**Ellen C. Cohen**, PhD, LMHC psychotherapist, New York City

CONTENTS

ACKNOWLEDGEMENTS

We thank our teachers, whose research and wisdom continue to inform, inspire and support us: Sharon Salzburg, Rick Hanson, Marshall Rosenberg, Laurel Mellin, Stephen Porges and Dan Siegel, and appreciate the support from Cinnie Noble, Dr. Ben Hoffman, Craig Runde and Pete Sperling. Thank you to our wonderful illustrator, Shoshanna Freedman.

We thank our family, friends and all of our clients who have taught us so much and mean the world to us.

Most of all we thank you, the reader, whose interest in this work means we share a desire for staying in balance and true to ourselves, learning tools to kind-heartedly co-exist or at least practice respectful tolerance, and solving problems in compassionate, wise and mature manners.

"Emotional strength develops out of your openness and willingness to tolerate, face, bear, and know as much of your moment-to-moment experience as possible."

—Dr. Joan Rosenberg

Why did we write this book?

Have you ever had one of those conversations you thought was going along fine, but then all of a sudden something went very wrong? You began to get upset, or the other person got upset. You no longer felt understood, a disagreement or struggle began, and you started to feel awful.

Or how about those conversations that seem to be about one thing, something fairly easy to discuss, but you can tell that there is something beneath the surface that isn't getting expressed? Suddenly tempers flare or difficult feelings begin to bubble forth.

Somehow the moment becomes difficult—it's hard to hear the other person or you don't feel heard and understood. Or maybe you lose touch with your intention, and forget what you wanted to say and why you wanted to say it in the first place. Perhaps you get swamped with negative feelings, or maybe the other person's negative feelings throw you into a panic.

Whether they're about work, family or the weather, we are all engaging in conversations every day, and many days we might be involved in hundreds of small conversations. Most of the time conversations are easy. However, inevitably there are conversations that hijack our calm, causing us to lose touch with our goals and our message, and resulting in stress and pain.

These are the tough conversations that can cause us to disconnect from ourselves and the other person. They can damage relationships and shared goals, and they can leave scars that are difficult to heal.

Hold On To Yourself offers a simple explanation of the science behind this universal experience and provides easy to use tools to help you stay connected to yourself when communication gets rough.

When we say hold on to yourself, we mean stay in your own body and experience—feel your feelings, trust your instincts, value yourself, and honor your differences. Staying cool means staying in homeostasis or balance, recognizing when things are getting tense and stressful, and using tools to help move you back to an open mind and an open heart, able to listen, speak clearly and creatively problem solve.

Without tools to support us during difficult conversations, it's easy to fall into less satisfying relationships, robbing us of the happiness, vibrancy and well-being we all deserve.

But, if we learn to hang in there and express ourselves at these roughest of times, conversations can bring rich rewards of deeper intimacy and growth, as well as better solutions to difficult problems.

We now know the neuroscience behind this phenomenon of disconnecting from ourselves and others in stressful conversations. It is built into our brain's wiring. And fortunately, we now have the tools to help us stay in balance and minimize the pain and suffering that can come from stressful, out-of-balance conversations.

This book evolved from the extensive professional and personal experiences, struggles, teaching and learning that both authors have had while helping people stay connected to themselves in conflict and stress.

As a mental health expert, Judy has worked with individuals, couples and groups for over thirty years and has found a troubling pattern that seems to be universal. When the conversation gets rough, when there's something important to share or request—something that threatens the status quo or exposes vulnerabilities—most of us struggle. It's so easy to trigger each other. When we get triggered we can clam up, shut down, spin our wheels or over power the other speaker. Often, we give up and stop communicating honestly altogether.

As a mediator, executive coach and trainer, Julia has worked inside organizations for over twenty years. What she has seen over and over again is that during tough conversations it's normal to get triggered—defensive, angry, shut down, and avoidant. In conflict, we act in ways that may not be our usual selves. Emotions take over, despite our knowing better.

Julia wanted to understand more about this phenomenon and wanted to offer her clients ways to respond more effectively to the storm of reactions going on inside during tough conversations. Meeting Judy provided an opportunity to dive more deeply into the area of self-regulation and holding on to oneself.

When Julia and Judy met, they shared a passion to bring their combined expertise and knowledge to teach and create tools their clients and others could use in their everyday lives at home and at work.

The tools and techniques presented in this book are informed by and adapted from a variety of sources. These sources are as diverse as Marshall Rosenberg's nonviolent communication training, Jon Kabat Zinn's mindfulness based stress reduction program (and other mindfulness-based practices), Laurel Mellin's emotional brain training, Daniel Goleman's emotional intelligence work, Jeffrey Young's schema therapy, Fisher & Ury's interest-based negotiation, Dan Siegel's interpersonal neurobiology, John Gottman's couples communication skills, Stephen Porges polyvagal theory and general neuroscience, as well as the science of self-regulation and the art of conflict management.

This book presents practical tools anyone can follow to strengthen skills to stay balanced, focused and empathic even in the most difficult of conversations or conflicts. You will learn to identify what stress state you are in—and why that information is important in tough conversations.

You will learn tools to protect yourself from going into stress states which make it virtually impossible to stay in balance. You will practice new ways to approach difficult conversations.

Our goal is to help you stay connected to yourself and in balance—a place where you can maintain your self respect, your alignment with your message, and your openness to understanding the other person's feelings and needs during all conversations, no matter how difficult. That way, you can creatively problem solve and build positive, healthy relationships to move you forward in your life in what Julia Cameron calls "good, orderly, direction."

The bottom line is that you matter. Your balance, peace and joy matter, and you can learn tools and build skills that will help you to stay more connected to your wisdom and heart.

What we have learned over the past fifty years of combined experience is that the more we can stay connected to our hearts and our wiser self—and communicate from that tender but powerful place—the more others, too, can begin to experience more joy, more connection and more positive resolutions to conflict. Not always, of course (and we'll be talking about that too), but it increases the likelihood of better outcomes for all.

CHAPTER 1

WHY IS IT SO HARD TO HOLD ON TO YOURSELF?

*"One can choose to go back toward safety or forward
toward growth. Growth must be chosen again and again;
fear must be overcome again and again."*
—Abraham Maslow

Conflict Myths Keep us Stuck

Imagine a life without any tough conversations, where you get up in the morning and go to bed at night with no struggles, no challenges, no difficulties in communication or relationships. Your boss and your co-workers are always supportive in every situation, your family members love every little thing you do, and everyone is always agreeing with you!

If this seems like a pipe dream compared to your life, you're not alone. A life completely empty of conflict is the life of either a miraculously advanced and spiritually evolved individual or a person who is isolated, numbed out or firmly situated in a too-comfortable comfort zone.

For most of us, life won't let us stay isolated, numbed out, or stuck in a safe place for very long. We have children, bosses, partners, neighbors, colleagues, clients and customers who force us to respond in ways that make us learn, change and grow.

That's what conflict and tough conversations are all about.

Yet, it's easy to believe wistful myths about conflict. Myths are beliefs that a whole group of people hold. That's what makes myths so hard to see: when most people around you agree with your view of reality, the status quo usually remains in place. Bumping into differences challenges beliefs and even our sense of identity; that's what makes them so threatening.

However, conflict also forces us to examine the beliefs we are comfortable holding and keeping in place and provides an opportunity for our beliefs to evolve into something richer and more expansive.

There are four common conflict myths that serve to blind us to conflict's potential for personal growth. These myths become most apparent when we're upset or having a tough conversation.

Here they are. See if any sound familiar to you. They reflect the conflict styles work by Blake and Mouton, Thomas-Kilmann, Kraybill and others:

- **Accommodating myth**: Conflict is bad because it destroys relationships, so I'd better be nice to you or else our relationship will be ruined.
- **Competing myth:** If there's conflict, I'm usually right, and you are wrong. That is, I usually win or, if I'm unlucky, I'll lose. Either way, conflict is a dog-eat-dog proposition.
- **Avoiding myth:** Conflict is so negative. It's scary and destructive and it shouldn't even exist. If we just ignore it hopefully it will go away.
- **Compromising myth:** What's the big deal? Everybody should be able to resolve conflict quickly and efficiently. We just all need to give a little and take a little. There's no real winner in conflict, but there's no real loser either.

Did you recognize any of these beliefs? Did any remind you of anyone influential in your life? A parent perhaps, or a sibling? Maybe you adopted one of these myths, or there was a message you heard and rejected.

These four myths can keep us stuck in the conflict-is-bad fable. Depending on how strongly you believe any one of them, seeing conflict and tough conversations as natural, healthy and vital for our growth can seem unimaginable.

Yet, deciding to see conflict as holding potential for change, growth, and even healing can actually help you stay cool in the face of it.

The root of the word "conflict" means "to rub up against." If we have active lives we are rubbing up against others on a regular basis. Tough conversations are built into the fabric of life, and without them, we wouldn't stretch ourselves beyond our habits.

In Buddhist psychology, conflicts or difficult conversations are considered to be our "Buddha on the path." They are where we get to test our assumptions and perceptions, our goals and our values. Conflict helps us more clearly define ourselves and the meaning we give to our life. It's how we build intimacy and connection, how we relate and share our lives with each other.

To help shift from that comfortable place, which is often born from fear of conflict, let's start with some metaphors to help re-imagine conflict, and hold it in a different light.

Here are some metaphors that may represent your current ideas of the conflict myths:

- **Accommodating:** Conflict is a wind storm—you adjust and change yourself to adapt.
- **Competing:** Conflict is a war—everyone has something to win or lose.
- **Avoiding:** Conflict is the black plague—to be avoided at all costs.
- **Compromising:** Conflict is a minor squalor—to be dealt with quickly and efficiently.

Now here are three new metaphors for healthy conflict. Consider each of them in turn:

1) Conflict is like a dance. What is my part in the dance?
2) Conflict is like white-river kayaking. What can I do to enjoy the ride?
3) Conflict is like standing in the eye of the storm. Where is the calm center?

Notice what you think and how you feel as you consider what your own images for conflict might be, and what a newer image could do for you.

What stories do you tell about conflict, and how could a new image create a new story?

Conflict Makes Us Feel Threatened

If tough conversations and conflict are "normal," if they help us grow and learn, if they are good for us, then why do we want to avoid them at all costs? Why do we have that tendency to fall into them without being able to find a way out? Why do we want to hang on to our conflict myths?

First, depending on how you view conflict, tough conversations can very quickly cause you to feel threatened. The threat comes from multiple sources. If you identify with one or more of the conflict myths or images we talked about, then feeling a threat response can happen fairly quickly.

You might also feel threatened in tough conversations because something important is at stake for you.

For example, the conversation may threaten the status quo in a relationship. It may bring up questions of your value or worth. It might open up perspectives that are difficult to embrace. Tough conversations are invariably loaded with emotional charge. They can feel risky, confusing or disturbing.

In conflict, something is on the line. Tough conversations make us feel vulnerable. We fear we could lose something important, like our job or our relationship. Something could change that would lead us into new, undefined and therefore scary territory. We might hurt or disappoint someone. We might be hurt or disappointed ourselves. We may be judged, disrespected, rejected or ignored.

One way or another, tough conversations imply a perception of a conscious or unconscious threat to your safety. In other words, they imply STRESS.

The Conflict and Stress Loop

Tough conversations, threat and stress are all woven together in a loop. When we are bringing up something difficult, or when we are suddenly confronted with a tough conversation, we get stressed. Stress causes us to lose hold of our sense of self—our most precious asset in conflict.

Fortunately, it is the neurobiology of stress that will ultimately help guide us, giving us the tools and strength to bring up the most difficult topics that are key to our greater good and happiness.

When you are feeling relaxed and well, when you are in balance, you probably feel pretty good about yourself and your life. You are fairly clear about your goals and intentions, and you can listen to others openly, as well as share your own thoughts and feelings. This is your brain in balance—minimally stressed, moving through your day with minimal upset.

But as your stress hormones get activated, your brain will change. Your thoughts will become more anxious, critical, judgmental, negative, or black-and-white. Your negative feelings will either ramp up or shut off completely, leaving you numb. You will be lost in your ruminative, busy thoughts.

Your interactions will also become more negative. The tonal quality of your voice will subtly change, your facial muscles will tense, your pupils will constrict, and others communicating with you will unconsciously mirror these subtle shifts, becoming stressed themselves.

You don't have a lot of control over this. It's not your choice; it's your neurobiology.

The challenge becomes this. When you are in conflict, you are stressed. When you are stressed, you are more likely to get into conflict. Conflict triggers the stress response. The stress response triggers conflict. When in stress, our brain shuts down and changes in ways that tend to make us dig deeper into the hole of conflict and stress. We activate others' stress response as well. Unconscious negative loops and patterns arise.

Does stress start conflict or does conflict start stress? Trying to sort that out is like trying to sort out which came first, the chicken or the egg. Ultimately, it doesn't matter. What matters is to remember that stress and conflict are linked, and that you can start to look at your conflicts through the lens of stress.

If you accept that stress and conflict go together, then you can avoid creating additional unnecessary conflict. By becoming more aware of what stress state you are in, you can make different choices in conflict.

Remember: *it's not you. It's not them. It's our shared neurobiology.* It bears repeating, because we tend to harshly judge ourselves and others when we are in stress.

We Don't Recognize Our Brain as an Operating System

To understand what happens to you and others during conflict, it is important to understand our neurobiology: the mechanics of our brain and what happens as stress mounts. It helps to learn the language of the brain in balance, a brain that can feel compassion, joy and connection; a brain that can communicate with empathy and focus. And finally, it is important to learn the language of stress, and how it impacts your communication.

With a brief training on your "operating system" you'll start to understand how to better take care of yourself, how to stay centered and connected, and how to hold on to yourself during tough conversations.

One thing to note, most researchers suggest that the brain is a series of very complex systems, and no structure operates alone. Also, there has been ongoing debate for decades about whether we have free will, consciousness, or a mind and whether everything is driven by our brain. This overview of the brain and its operating system is not meant to answer these larger philosophical questions. What we will be sharing with you is a simplified version of the latest information coming out of fMRI (functional magnetic resonance imaging) research relating to how the brain functions in balance and in stress. These findings are of practical use, regardless of larger, more complex topics about the brain.

To start, take a look at this list of some of the brain's operating hardware that get activated and play a part in our response to tough conversations. We will not dive into all aspects of the brain in this book. However, this overview serves to highlight how much biological action is going on during tough conversations. These are not "childish" reactions. These are normal areas of the brain creating normal biochemical activities built into our neurobiology as humans:

- **The Amygdala** (fear/anger center) is part of our more primitive mammalian brain. The amygdala is our own little "homeland security system" and fuels our fight, flight, freeze or submit response. Early trauma or difficulties can sensitize our amygdala and makes us more apt to be stressed in conflict. This is reflected in how some of us seem to generally get more stressed more easily than others.

- **The Prefrontal Cortex** (thinking center or PFC) helps focus our attention and plan what we will do or say. The PFC narrates situations and creates stories from experience, as well as helps orchestrate thoughts and actions. The PFC goes "offline" in the stress response. That is, in a full-blown stress response, we do not have much access to this part of our more "rational" thinking brain.

- **The Hippocampus** (context center) interprets information coming in from the amygdala and sends messages to the prefrontal cortex. It helps "reframe" our initial fear or anger, and puts our experience in context. The hippocampus is impacted by stress and depression, trauma and anxiety. Stress, and the other emotional states mentioned, can literally shrink the dendrites (a neuron's receivers) in the hippocampus, giving us less access to reframe our initial, more primitive responses.

- **The Reward System** (approach/avoidance center) is a set of structures in the brain that light up when we have moments of warmth and connection, or pleasure and good feelings. The reward system also lights up when we are in stress and deliver a "zinger" comment, or otherwise make a "victorious" action. We want to go towards those things that feel good and move away from those things that seem painful, like facing a tough conversation.

- **The Vagus Nerve** (communication center) "wanders" from the midbrain to the belly and sends messages from the brain to the heart and the gut and then back up to the brain, as well as linking the brain and body movements. The Vagal Brake ("on" and "off" center) is a term that refers to the messages sent through our vagus nerve. When our "vagal brake" is off, we are on the fast track into the stress response; we are no longer able to adequately connect with another person, to listen, or to understand. A vagal brake that is "on" allows us to feel empathy, to listen actively, and to creatively problem solve. If you practice the tools you learn in this book, you will be strengthening your vagal brake.

- **The Basal Ganglia** (habit center) learns what "typical" patterns of interaction are and takes over whenever stress mounts and the more primitive parts of our brain are triggered. Our habit-based patterns in communication and behavior are run by these structures. Our more ingrained responses come out during stress. These patterns in stress show how our habitual thinking patterns are "wired."

- **Survival Circuitry** (fight/flight/freeze/submit center) gets activated when we feel threatened, and a whole cavalcade of hormones and neurochemicals get released. We are in survival mode. Stress activates survival circuitry.

- **Implicit Memory** (unconscious schema and emotional memory center) refers to our unconscious memory, which can get triggered in an instant if the brain perceives a threat. Our autobiographical memory is what we can talk about: "First I did this, and then that happened..." However, we can't really discuss our implicit memory, as it is housed in our emotional or unconscious brain. But the brain remembers, and the stronger the original emotion embedded in memory, the more associations we may have with the original emotions and the stronger the reaction will be.

- **Bottom Up versus Top Down Processing** refers to two general ways our brain can process incoming information. *Bottom-up* means the emotional brain, or more primitive brain structures are involved: we are processing from the bottom of our brain, up to our logical levels. When this happens, our communication skills are limited. *Top-down* processing means that we are able to access our wisdom, our compassion, and the more highly evolved parts of our brain. With top-down processing, our PFC is online so we can more easily access our communication tools and skills. With bottom up processing, no matter how skilled and educated we are, no matter how high-minded our intention, our tools and skills can go down the drain in a moment.

- **Default Mode Network** refers to our brain's "chatter"—meaning the nearly constant stream of thoughts that swim about in our minds as we go about our day. Buddhists call this "monkey mind." When you meditate, you can observe this stream of thoughts. Much of this stream is "self-referencing," meaning thoughts about ourselves. Much of this stream is below or at the edge of our conscious awareness.

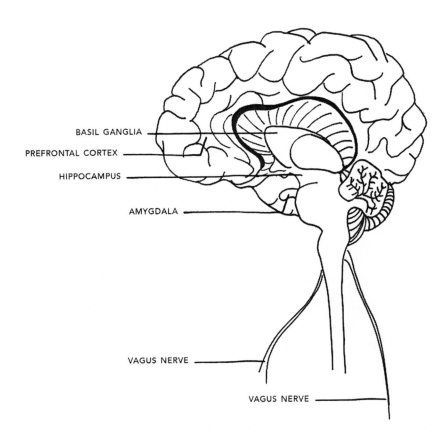

BASIL GANGLIA

PREFRONTAL CORTEX

HIPPOCAMPUS

AMYGDALA

VAGUS NERVE

VAGUS NERVE

We Disconnect From Ourselves and Others

When you are humming along in balance, when your brain gets a sense that "all is well" and there is not a threat or danger in the environment, your stress hormones will be less active, your vagal brake will more likely be in its "on" position, your implicit memories will be silent and submerged, and you will be more likely to operate with top-down processing.

You can stay connected to yourself in conversation, and stay present and balanced enough to be creative in problem solving, to listen with empathy, and to move toward resolving difficulties in positive, healthy ways.

But when you go into the stress response, your brain perceives a danger or threat. This perceived threat can be triggered from the outside environment, or from the inside—a thought you are having, a sensation of tension or anxiety, an emotion that arises, or even just being hungry.

Your stress hormones get ramped up, your vagal brake goes off, you begin bottom-up processing, and your early emotional experiences (implicit memories) are likely to be triggered, coming to the surface and impacting your thoughts, feelings and behaviors.

Stress responses can get triggered in an instant. This is good! Imagine the times you need to slam on the brakes or grab your child when he is running into the busy street. Think of the times you have a tight deadline and have to operate at full throttle. Chances are the stress response has saved your life a few times over the years and helped you be more productive and efficient.

Unfortunately, the stress response can also get triggered in a millisecond when you're in a conversation, especially a tough conversation with an important other person; someone with whom you feel some interdependence, or someone you believe has influence, meaning, and power in your world.

So, let's say you are talking with your spouse about sex or money, or asking your boss for a raise, or bringing up a tough topic on caring for your elderly parent with your sister. You may start off OK, but something gets triggered, and before you know it your heart rate is up, your hormones are activated, and you've plummeted right into stress.

You've gone from top-down processing to bottom-up processing.

When your stress hormones are coursing through your blood stream, it makes it impossible to stay on point with your message and engaged in listening. It's impossible to feel compassionate towards yourself and others, or to stay open, positive, and connected in order to creatively solve problems.

You lose hold of yourself.

Our Stress Level Impacts our Thoughts, Feelings and Behaviors

In the stress response your personality, as well as your physical experience, actually changes. There are a whole host of neurobiological activities that are making the chemistry in your body react. You know the sayings "That makes my blood boil" or "My heart was racing" or "I felt a pit in my stomach." These are our way of expressing that mind-body connection. These are the ways we describe our physiological reactions to stress.

We all exhibit behavioral tendencies when stressed that are not our favorite tendencies. Here are the kinds of behaviors we can engage in when we are stressed:

- Blaming
- Getting critical and judgmental
- Feeling out of control
- Getting angry
- Feeling guilt or shame
- Feeling panicky or anxious
- Falling into a rigid or stuck point of view
- Obsessively thinking and getting into "thought loops"
- Losing touch with our own needs, the other person's needs, or both
- Getting lost in the interpersonal dynamic and losing touch with our intentions
- Feeling powerless and less-than, or trying to overpower and feeling greater-than

We have lost our connection with our message, our self, and the other person. We're "in the jungle," fighting for our lives. In this state the primitive, more reactive parts of our brain have taken over. We are out-of-balance, and often don't even realize it.

Stress Triggers Early Schemas

The brain is designed to organize patterns of thought, experience and behavior to simplify and codify learning and experience quickly and efficiently. The term *schemas* refer to these organized patterns. Unfortunately, our early schemas can be faulty and destructive and can get triggered in stress.

This primitive part of our brain, which gets triggered in stress, has a massive unconscious component that was largely wired when we were little. In fact about 70% of our brain is already developed by the time we are three. We pick up early associations that lead to false beliefs and expectations about ourselves, others and life. These early associations are schemas, and can become an ingrained pattern that stays below our conscious awareness, stored in our "implicit memory." These memories rise up and take charge when we're in stress.

This is why it is so easy to get stuck in patterns of interaction with your spouses, siblings, bosses, or co-workers. The patterns are unconscious; they pop up in stress when you are most vulnerable, and they literally force you to behave according to old scripts.

If a current conversation happens to touch upon an old hurt or early learning you can plummet into the full-blown stress response in an instant. These schemas are "touchy"—meaning they are neural circuits that can be highly sensitive and easily aroused.

That's why if something touches you deeply and quickly, if you have strong feelings or find yourself reacting almost uncontrollably, chances are it's revealing a schema.

Up goes your heart rate, blood pressure and body temperature as if you were being attacked by a predator, and all you are doing is trying to politely ask for a raise. Or ask your spouse to do the dishes more often. Or give your team members feedback about the team's communication.

12

We Split from our Wise Self

Once the primitive biology of stress has taken over, the conversation tends to be a lost cause. That's when the brain tends to "split." Your wise and perceptive prefrontal cortex goes offline and your emotional brain takes over. Your thinking tends to get negative, biased, blaming, shaming, obsessive or defensive. Your feelings will get ramped up: you'll be angry, furious, rageful or you may find yourself plummeting into hopeless and helpless, powerless feelings. You can feel shame, panic, anxiety. For some of us, feelings tend to shut off and we'll become numb, paralyzed and disoriented.

In other words, our choices are:

1. **Fight**: we get angry, irritated, frustrated, annoyed, or criticize. We judge harshly and condemn.
2. **Flight:** we get panicked, feel terror, anxiety, or fear, and hide by saying we didn't care about the issue after all. We create distance, run away, and do whatever is necessary to escape.
3. **Freeze**: we get numb, paralyzed, frozen, distant, hopeless, or despairing.
4. **Submit**: we get deferential, obsequious, feel "less-than," give way to the other.

Stress hormones take over our reason, our wisdom and our heart. Our adult, rational and wise brain has been hijacked. The out-of-control kids are in charge.

These reactions are biological and perfectly normal.

It helps to remember this is just our normal, human wiring, as chances are you tend to harshly judge yourself and others when you get into these out-of-balance brain states.

Judging yourself or others for this biological hijacking not only makes matters worse by fueling more stress and keeping you in stuck patterns, but it's an inaccurate perception. If you could do better in that moment, you would. You don't have complete control over your stress biology. We all have primitive reactions when old wounds are touched upon. It's perfectly normal.

That's not to say it's appropriate to react as if the other person really is a saber-tooth tiger; only that it can happen, and often does happen, to all of us.

We Can't Hear

To add another ingredient to this recipe for conversational disaster, when we are in the stress response we will not be able to hear the other person. Our own thoughts, feelings and body sensations tend to get so loud inside us that we really can't hear or understand what they're saying. Again, this is biological. It's not that we are bad, immature or selfish people. It's that our primitive jungle biology is activated and we are hooked by our survival circuitry.

Biologically, when in the stress response, that bottom up processing we've discussed gets triggered, your vision literally narrows and your focus gets acute and stuck. Your hearing, too, can be impacted. You may no longer be able to truly listen; your own thoughts become predominant and repetitive and your brain begins "tuning out" the other speaker. Sometimes your brain starts over-focusing on the other and "tunes out" you! Thinking outside of the box becomes impossible.

We're Stuck in Stress

Often in stress we simply try to keep hammering to get our point across, escalating our intensity or voice in hope that the other person will hear us, or shut down, give up and fume. These options tend to further exacerbate the situation and our own stress.

In less stressed times your hippocampus puts your fear or anger into context by reminding you that you are safe and it's only your spouse or your boss, not a terrorist or tiger that you're dealing with. But in the stress response, the hippocampus can't seem to put the threat into context. The communication link between your amygdala and PFC is snagged. Your empathy and understanding has gone cold as the "vagal brake" turns off and your body is cued to run, attack, freeze or submit.

Your implicit memory systems, located deep in the emotional brain, are getting activated and it's not pretty—you're unconsciously or semi-consciously remembering all the past injuries, arguments, losses, embarrassment, and pain. Remember your implicit memory refers to the unconscious emotional material from the past, where your brain may have made faulty assumptions or conclusions about yourself, others and life.

Current situations that feel threatening to the brain, even if it's just a slight blow to your self-esteem, or a suggestion of a mistake or a subtle doubt about your value or worthiness, can trigger a whole set of these implicit memories or faulty expectations and assumptions.

No wonder these conversations tend to go straight down the tube and rapidly too!

One thing to emphasize: getting stuck in this stress response happens to all of us. Even if you have a PhD in Communication, are a therapist or a mediator, you will find yourself losing hold of yourself in certain tough conversations. You may learn skills to cover it up, to make it look like you're listening by nodding and staying engaged, but inside you may be feeling self-righteous, frustrated, anxious or deflated.

Putting it into Practice: Three Conflict Images and Three Beliefs

Here's the wonderful and hopeful news. You can break out of the box of your own stress response and the repetitive patterns in your life. You can rewire your brain to be more resilient to stress, and to stay cool in hot conversations. You can learn to help your brain move from bottom-up to top-down processing.

And the best part of learning these skills and building your stress resilience is this: when you hold on to yourself, when you return to above the line processing, you can feel your own strength, goodness and wisdom. You can feel empathy and warmth towards others. You can be open to creative problem solving and win-win solutions. You can move forward in your life, with intention, heart and spirit. All it takes is tools and practice!

Three Conflict Images

It starts with how you see conflict. Do you see it as a war or can you see it as a dance? Is it to be avoided like the plague or can it be an exhilarating challenge like white water rafting? Is it a minor issue to be solved quickly or can there be an advantage to staying with the conflict like riding in the eye of a storm?

Which image would you like to start to associate with conflict? Pick one now.

Three Conflict Beliefs

Here are three key beliefs about conflict that can serve to strengthen the connection between stress, conflict and growth. These beliefs will help to reconnect your stressed out self with your wiser self. These realizations will be obscured by the stress response, so as you read these, see if you can feel the truth about each one and see how they fit into your experience. Memorize and practice them so they will be more accessible in the heat of the moment. When you are triggered, access these beliefs to help you soothe and reconnect with yourself.

1) Zero conflict is a myth: Don't blame myself or others!

When in stress, we tend to think in terms of all-or-nothing, good or bad, right or wrong, black-and-white. This is the brain splitting and is an evolutionarily based survival strategy. Our prefrontal cortex splits from our primitive brain and we disconnect from our wisdom and wider perspective in order to react faster to threats. We don't want to over think whether we should slam on the brakes. It's normal, it's built into our wiring, it's important to our survival as a species. So, practicing this statement can help remind you that you (and the other person too, perhaps) are slipping into a way of thinking and responding that is not your best self. It's natural. It happens. Do not blame yourself or the other person.

16

2) **Conflict is natural, healthy and vital for growth: Don't believe or act on your stress-based thoughts!**

In stress, your brain loses its capacity to think "outside the box" or creatively. Your hippocampus shuts down and your implicit memories start lighting up. Old, unconscious patterns present themselves in how you think, feel, behave and how you communicate.

Do not believe what you are thinking when your brain is out-of-balance, and don't take to heart what another is saying in these stressed states. You do not WANT to be speaking this way or feeling this way. This isn't your heart's intention any more than it is the other's!

3) **Conflict is an opportunity to learn more about myself and the other: Be prepared for childish or primitive reactions, and look deeper.**

The more we judge, blame, criticize or think negatively about ourselves, another person, a situation or a conflict, the more vulnerable we are to going into the stress response and sealing in the negative conditions. We can get stuck in a negative loop or repetitive patterns in our key relationships.

Reminding yourself that you are being challenged to stretch and learn in those difficult times can be self-soothing. It will be difficult to see in the moment, so it's useful to remind yourself of this way of looking at conflict. As Maslow reminds us, we *can choose to go back toward safety or forward toward growth*!

Conflict is an opportunity for discovery. Practice releasing blame and judgment during stressful, difficult conversations. Remind yourself that stress-based thoughts are faulty and are not to be trusted. Remember that conflict is normal and healthy and essential to growth. By practicing these key beliefs you'll be deepening your self- awareness as well as your sensitivity to the other person. This will strengthen your ability to resolve problems more creatively.

In the next chapter, we'll describe three internal states to be aware of so you can start to notice when you or another person is beginning to get out-of-balance and move into stress.

CHAPTER 2

TO SIMPLIFY: THREE STATES

"The human brain...is the most complexly organised structure in the universe and to appreciate this you just have to look at some numbers. The brain is made up of one hundred billion nerve cells or "neurons" which is the basic structural and functional units of the nervous system. Each neuron makes something like a thousand to ten thousand contacts with other neurons and these points of contact are called synapses where exchange of information occurs. And based on this information, someone has calculated that the number of possible permutations and combinations of brain activity, in other words the numbers of brain states, exceeds the number of elementary particles in the known universe."

—V.S. Ramachandran

In our first chapter, we introduced the stress response and how it impacts us in conflict. One key point is that our stress biology impacts our response to conflict and our response to conflict impacts our stress biology. So, increasing our awareness of our inner experience and stress level is important if we want to stay cool in conflict.

It's easy to fall into chronic busy or numbed-out states, where we don't know whether or not we are stressed unless it's really obvious. By the time it's really obvious, it's often too late to catch ourselves in a place where it's easier to handle.

In this chapter, we are going to move deeper inside ourselves. You will learn about the more subtle aspects of the stress states so you can recognize the signs within yourself and support yourself through your own response. To hold on to yourself when the going gets tough, you need to strengthen your awareness of the "you" that you are holding on to.

Three States Described

Because our brains are such complex systems, each moment is a unique choreography of electrical charges and impulses, chemical releases and speed-of-light transactions. To simplify, we'd like to suggest that at any given moment, based on a whole lot of factors beyond our control, our brain is in one of three states. We've named these three states: balanced, triggered and out-of-balance:

1. **Balanced**—This is a state of general well-being. Here the brain has minimal stress hormones operating, and you are in a state of "neural integration," which means your hemispheres are communicating, your pre-frontal cortex is online, and you are processing information and experience in healthy ways. You can speak openly and with compassion. You are connected to yourself and to the other person. You feel free to share your ideas, feelings and needs, and listen to the other person's perspective with understanding. This is when you are feeling secure, worthy, respectful, connected and balanced. This is a homeostatic state of well-being and joy.

2. **Triggered**—This state signifies that your brain has perceived a threat, and your stress hormones and neurochemicals are beginning to be triggered. Your focus, feelings, and thoughts, as well as your body's physiology, automatically begin to change. You are moving into the stress response. In this inner state, your stress hormones may cause you to begin to doubt yourself, and you may have feelings like worry, fear, anger or guilt. When these feelings arise you may begin to feel unsafe.

    In this state it's harder to listen to the other person. You may begin to judge the other or to defend yourself. You may begin to get trapped in your own thoughts and inner arguments. You are starting to perceive threats; threats to identity, to self esteem, to point of view, to security, or even to your very life. Your body and conditioning are beginning to take over. You are moving toward your unconscious, fight/flight/freeze/submit posture.

3. **Out-of-balance**—This is the state where your stress hormones and neurochemicals have ramped up so you are lost in your fight/flight/freeze/submit reactions. Feelings are either completely ramped up or completely shut down, depending on your survival tendencies. When you are in this state, you can no longer even hear what another person is saying. You're no longer rational, so there is no point trying to pretend that you are or to try to keep the conversation going. You've forgotten your intention, values and sometimes even your message and are instead caught in a past memory loop. Your thoughts are going to be negative, judging, blaming, repetitive, and tunnel-visioned. These kinds of behaviors, in yourself or others, are signs that your fight/flight/freeze/submit response is fully activated. Your usual loving and caring self is no longer home!

Identify Your State

Being able to identify which state you are in is very useful. The stress state you are in impacts your thoughts, feelings and behaviors.

The following charts describe some of the tendencies people have in thought, feeling and behavior in the three states. These tendencies are fairly universal, but we all hold a unique thumbprint when it comes to stress reactions. Familiarize yourself with these to see if you can recognize any.

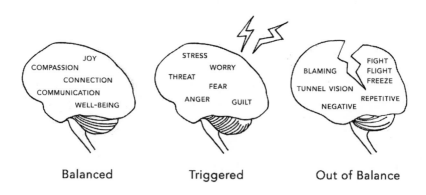

Balanced   Triggered   Out of Balance

The Three States Summary

State 1: Balanced

Thoughts	Feelings	Behaviors
Positive, reasonable, optimistic, solution-focused, empathic, balanced. "We can solve this" "We both matter"	Balanced, hopeful, relaxed, open, real, present, peaceful, compassionate, whole, engaged, aware, flowing, connected	Thoughtful, balanced, connecting, healthy, wise, adult, sensitive, aware, conscious

State 2: Triggered

Thoughts	Feelings	Behaviors
Tentative, cautious, urgent, upset, questioning, doubting "This isn't working," "He is not getting it"	Concerned, anxious, worried, irritated, annoyed, bored, tuning out, confused, blank, frustrated, upset	Faster speech, louder, turning away, shutting down, distracted, losing track, beginning to numb (cravings, distractions, etc...)

State 3: Out-of-balance

Thoughts	Feelings	Behaviors
Blaming, repetitive, critical, rigid, irrational, reactive, obsessed, extreme, "What a jerk," "I'm not good enough," "I give up"	Overwhelmed, numb, ramped up negative feelings, rage, fury, shame, extremism, shut down, aggressive, powerless, disoriented, confounded	Faster speech, louder, destructive, abrupt, mean, punitive, self abusive, unconscious, demeaning, hurtful to self and others

Raising Your Stress Set Point

One of the challenges of modern life is this: we are designed for periodic bouts of physical stress, but in our Western or Westernized cultures we tend to have chronic emotional stress. Chronic stress states can change the structure and function of our brain, resulting in a "set point." The more time we spend in stress, either triggered or full-blown stress, the more easily our brain will "go there."

We all know people who seem to be stuck in negative perspectives and hopeless thoughts, or who are trapped in depressed, anxious, or blaming and judgmental states. (In fact, we all probably have been there ourselves at one time or another).

This really means that they are stuck in the stress response. They may only have periodic bounces up to a balanced state, or homeostasis, where they feel happy, grateful feelings and connect meaningfully. Unfortunately, when we have a stressed "set point" our brain may bounce to joy and homeostasis, but it doesn't stay there long.

Luckily, you don't have to stay stuck in negative stress states. You can raise your stress set point and feel more joy, balance and connection in your life. To be able to raise your stress set point and have more resilience to deal with conflict, it helps first to be aware of what state you tend to fall into. Once you do, you can then strengthen your ability to hold on to yourself.

What We Mean by Hold On To Yourself

Holding on to yourself in difficult conversations means that you have developed enough self-awareness to notice when your state is changing from balanced to triggered. In that state, you have more choices about what you can do to rebalance yourself. Holding on to yourself also means noticing when you, or another, have moved into that out-of-balance state. That's a full-blown stress response. It's not the time to keep talking. That's not the right strategy when people are that upset. Increasing our self-awareness about what state we are in, enables us to choose the right strategy for the right brain state.

It is only when you have enough awareness to notice when you lose your grip on yourself in the first place, however, that you can take any steps to bring yourself back to a more balanced state.

That's where we will start.

The next chapters will help you take a closer look at patterns like merging and distancing in your personal stress response, and will introduce the tools and techniques you can use to strengthen your inner calm and keep you moving in a healthy, self-supporting direction in your relationships, your career and your life.

CHAPTER 3

WE DISCONNECT IN STRESS

"Differentiation means the capacity to be an 'I' while remaining connected."

—*Edwin Friedman*

This chapter will explain secure attachment, the vagus nerve, and the importance of vagal braking habits. We will show you how conflict, or a sense of disconnection, fuels stress for all social mammals; creatures who are wired for inter-connection. We will also explain the patterns of merging and distancing, which can be an automatic, reactive part of your stress response.

Look for your own tendencies in any of these patterns. They are normal, but not necessarily adaptive, meaning they are not best for your health and happiness. Learning about your tendencies helps you move to secure attachment, even in stressful situations.

Wired for Tribal Closeness

First, it is important to understand the role social connections play in our stress response. We are designed to live and work in teams, tribes, groups and communities. Our physical and emotional health requires connection to others. From infancy these connections build our security and positive balance.

We are wired for connection to ourselves, our families and communities, nature, pets and animals, and life in general. We are wired for a transcendent, spiritual longing or desire to connect with something greater than ourselves.

A healthy attunement to caregivers early in life and a healthy connection to self and others lead to what's called "secure attachment." The securely attached individual will be better at self-regulation, emotional balance, and handling conflict.

When we say stay cool in conflict we are basically saying stay securely attached to yourself no matter how rocky the road in relationships and communication.

Conflict and Disconnection

As social mammals, we are wired for connection. Like other social mammals, our primitive neurobiology is wired to be in balance when we feel like we have a safe place in our "tribe;" when we feel safely connected to others and feel like part of a community.

If we feel threatened it can trigger our most primitive stress responses. We might feel as if we do not belong or will be left out of the tribe. If we feel like others are disconnecting from us with disagreement, judgment, rejection or anger, we can become defensive and stressed.

This stress response causes us to disconnect from others. This disconnection stimulates more stress for both us and the other person as we move further and further apart in conflict. Conflict and disconnection are symbiotically connected, and the road they use is the vagus nerve.

The Vagus Nerve

The vagus nerve is a long wandering nerve traveling all the way from the mid-brain region to the gut. It has many branches along the way that veer out and connect with important organs, muscles and other nerves.

The vagus nerve helps coordinate facial expressions (nodding, smiles, etc...), which is key to establishing and maintaining social connections. The vagus nerve also controls the interaction between breathing, heart rate and your immune system, and regulates the "connection hormone," oxytocin, as well as other hormones. All of these physiological elements are important in staying balanced during social interactions.

Meanwhile, your unconscious thoughts, your amygdala, and your other more primitive brain structures are busy assessing, moment by moment, if you are safe or unsafe. These base instincts determine if you are interacting with a friend or a foe, or if there's a threat in the environment.

This unconscious assessment is part of your instant messaging system, communicating through your vagus nerve to all the organs and muscles in your body. It's a fundamentally simple communication. How safe or threatened am I? Do I need to turn on the fight, flight, freeze or submit response? Does my vagal brake need to be on or off?

When your vagal brake is *off*, your sympathetic nervous system kicks into gear. You plummet down into an out-of-balance and out-of-control stress response. Your heart rate goes up, your breathing gets fast and shallow; blood leaves your brain and belly to prepare your limbs for flight or fight, and muscles tense. You become anxious, angry, and upset. Your thoughts get narrowly focused, confused, blurry or repetitive. You interpret the moment as dangerous and threatening.

This sympathetic nervous response is what we are calling the out-of-balance, full blown stress state—you are not feeling safe.

When your vagal brake gets turned back *on*, the vagus nerve activates the parasympathetic response. The parasympathetic response is responsible for calming your physiology. Your heart rate slows down, your facial expression gets warm and inviting again, you feel kinder, gentler feelings. You can access empathy. You can listen. You can give and receive support, caring and love.

This is called the "sympathetic shift." It is what we are calling the state of homeostasis, or balance. The stronger our vagal response, the more compassion you can feel, as well as empathy and humanity. You can listen openly, you can problem-solve creatively, you can attune to the other and stay attuned to yourself.

Remember that the term "sympathetic" in this context refers to a physiological mechanism, not your personal intentions or character. A "sympathetic response" does not mean compassion, but rather a stimulation of the *sympathetic nervous system* located in the brain stem.

Studies show that we can develop a stronger "vagal brake" through meditation, exercise and personal growth practices. This is the rationale for the tools we'll be teaching you next. These are tools that will help strengthen your vagal brake, helping prevent and create more adaptive responses to stress.

Vagus Nerve Diagram

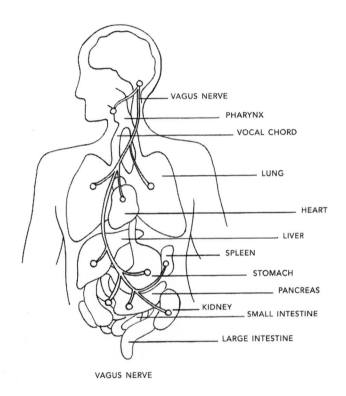

VAGUS NERVE

PHARYNX

VOCAL CHORD

LUNG

HEART

LIVER

SPLEEN

STOMACH

PANCREAS

KIDNEY

SMALL INTESTINE

LARGE INTESTINE

VAGUS NERVE

Vagal Superstars

Dacher Keltner, co-founder and faculty director of UC Berkley's Center for the Greater Good, has coined the term "vagal superstar." Vagal superstars have more positive emotions on a daily basis, stronger relationships with peers, and better social support networks. Studies have shown that fifth graders with a stronger vagal tone are more likely to intervene when they witness bullying, and they are more likely to give up recess when a fellow student needs help studying.

Vagal superstars can hold on to themselves in conflict and difficult situations. They are more resilient to interpersonal stress. The more you strengthen your vagal brake or what's called vagal "tone", the more you protect yourself from stress, and the more interpersonally effective you become. Here are some tips in what weakens, and what strengthens, your vagal tone.

Habits that Weaken the Vagal Brake

In our current culture it is very easy to fall into habits that can weaken your vagal brake. For instance, being on automatic pilot, or mindlessly going through your day weakens your vagal strength. If you deny, repress, or numb-out your feelings it can weaken the vagus response.

Using food, shopping or screen time to numb out are habits that weaken your vagal brake. Sedentary lifestyles, jobs without meaning or purpose, and violence in your communities or in the media weaken the vagus brake. Disconnection from yourself, others, nature and the spiritual also weaken the vagal brake.

The list of things that weaken your vagal tone goes on: too many choices or too few choices in your life, depressed and anxious feelings, difficult commutes, unhappy relationships, and general chronic unhappiness. All these factors can dampen the strength of your vagal brake and make you more vulnerable to stress, less compassionate, less happy and less satisfied in your life. All this makes you more likely to disconnect from yourself and others during difficult conversations. These are the reasons to adopt some habits that strengthen the vagal brake.

Here are some practical ways to increase your vagal tone.

Five Practices to Strengthen the Vagal Brake

There are many ways you can strengthen your vagal brake, making you more prepared for the inevitable conflict and stress that an engaged life brings. We have listed below five practices that you can do to strengthen your vagal brake. The more you practice these lessons in your daily life, the more they will become your new habits, building resilience to stress and creating a buffer so you can more easily hold on to yourself.

Lifestyle Practices: First, check in with your general lifestyle habits. Any activities that help curb stress can strengthen vagal tone. Exercise is the first one, which most of us know about, but don't necessarily practice often enough. Other common lifestyle practices that will strengthen your vagal brake are enjoying nature more often, playing with pets or children, engaging in caring acts for loved ones, making love, talking with friends, enjoying hobbies and activities, making things with your hands, eating nutritious food, and getting regular sleep.

All of these practices help strengthen the vagal brake. If any one (or several) of these are significantly off, they can increase stress and result in unnecessary and unproductive conflict. So, if you find yourself in a particularly conflicted time, look to your lifestyle habits. Are there some that you usually practice but recently have been too busy to keep up? Are there any that you could do more frequently?

Conflict takes a lot of inner strength and resources to deal with. The more you can take care of yourself, the stronger you will be in engaging conflict constructively.

Spiritual Practices: A second area that strengthens the vagal tone involves spiritual practices of all kinds. Prayer, meditation, journaling, inspiring reading, connection with spiritual communities, and honoring the grace and the mystery of life all contribute to a stronger vagal brake.

This may not be something that most people connect with tough conversations, but taking the time to reflect in a way that brings a broader perspective, having faith or belief in something bigger than oneself, and honoring the wonder in life can all help put tough conversations in perspective.

Gratitude Practices: You may be familiar with the power of gratitude, the third practice that helps strengthen vagal tone. Keeping a gratitude journal, listing a few things you are grateful for when you wake up in the morning or go to sleep at night, or just reflecting periodically on what you appreciate and what you feel good about in your life all have an impact on your vagal brake.

Creative Practices: Creative expression, including art, music and dance, all enrich vagal strength. Exploring what you love, what nourishes your soul or spirit, what brings you expanded feelings of awe and appreciation, and finding ways to create or express yourself are powerful enhancers of your vagal tone.

Mindfulness Practices: A fifth habit to help make for a healthy vagal tone is to strengthen your connection to your feelings, to your body, and to your breath. This practice of feeling your feelings, putting your awareness into your heart, or your belly or your breath, is a core tool for not only strengthening vagal tone but for mindfulness. Mindfulness is key in strengthening our vagal tone. We will go into more detail about this particular practice later in the book.

Having a stronger vagal brake is not something that can happen overnight. It is a commitment to live your life in a way that strengthens your connection to yourself, day to day. As your vagal brake strengthens, so too does your ability to deal with stress more effectively, and to engage in difficult conversations more productively. These general lifestyle habits, spiritual and appreciative practices, creative pursuits, and mindfulness habits are all aspects of living a life that is in a more balanced state more of the time.

Is there one habit you would like to bring into your daily living more? Which one would that be?

Survival-Based Relationship Patterns: Merging and Distancing

None of us will be able to avoid times when our vagal brake is off. The practices above simply help us decrease the frequency and intensity of our reactivity.

When those stressful moments and times arise and your vagal brake is off, your brain's priority becomes survival. These are the times you can easily move into survival-based relationship patterns. There are two basic survival-based relationship patterns: the drive to merge (becoming too close, losing connection with self) and the drive to distance (pushing away and losing connection with the other).

We learn these behavioral patterns in childhood, and they can get repeated throughout our important relationships.

Awareness Tool: Do I Merge, Distance or Both?

If you tend to merge or distance (or both) in tough conversations, then learning to create a stronger, healthier boundary will help you stay close and connected, while staying safe within your own skin and true to yourself and your message.

Here's a more detailed description of merging and distancing. See if either or both of these tendencies fit you. Once you have a better sense of your survival-based relationship pattern, you can pick a practice that suits your pattern.

Merging

> When conversations heat up your boundaries get very thin. You tend to get anxious. You focus on how the other person feels and what you need to do to please them or help them feel better. It feels threatening, not safe, to have someone near you unhappy or upset.

> You lose track of how you feel and what you need around others. You adapt yourself to take care of others in order to relieve stress. You morph, camouflage, discount or lose yourself in order to make them happy or resolve the tension. You are hyper-alert to others' feelings, and learn how to take care of or try to change others so you can feel safe.

When you merge you are trying to get your value, security, love, and safety from someone else. You try to fix, manipulate or control them so that they think well of you or aren't angry, disappointed or rejecting.

When you learn to merge to create a feeling of safety, conflict, or any negative feelings from another, can feel extremely threatening. Conflict can throw you into the full-blown stress response.

Merging Reflection Questions:

1. Do I tend to lose my connection with my own feelings, needs and ideas in more heated conversations?
2. Do I find myself wanting to please the other person, or acquiesce to their needs and perspective?
3. Am I uncomfortable with conflict and would rather not make my point then speak up loudly?
4. Do I get uncomfortable when other people have strong feelings, and I find myself bending over backwards to try to help them calm down or cool off?
5. Would I rather "go with the flow" then fight the current?
6. Do I end up feeling guilty or ashamed about my feelings and views if they are different than others? Do I end up feeling like I'm wrong or not good enough?

Distancing

When conversations heat up your boundaries get very thick. You become focused on how you feel, what you need and your own inner dialogue. You lose touch with how the other person feels and what they need. You can't really hear their thoughts, ideas or feelings. You are too busy over-focusing on yourself—your own thoughts, feelings and needs.

When you distance you tend to put up walls, judge, get angry or disengage. You get righteous, knowing you are "right" and they are "wrong." You discount them. You stop listening and get over-focused on your message and your need.

You might shut down, numb-out, give up or hide. You learned to get your safety by creating distance between yourself and others. You learned to disengage when conflict happens, to put up a wall, or check out.

Chances are you learned as a child to get your comfort, balance, and safety from pushing away from or escaping and avoiding others.

Distancing Reflection Questions:

1. Do I tend to know I'm right and wish other people would just see my point without discussion?
2. Does it make me mad or frustrated to have to listen to stupid ideas?
3. Do I tend to judge other people as not being smart enough, or too this or that? Do I tend to judge, resent or not like others?
4. Do I end up walking away in a huff when I don't get my way or don't feel heard?
5. Am I uncomfortable when other people have strong feelings, and do I tend to tell them to stop feeling that way?
6. Do I tend to feel angry or frustrated if people don't see my point of view? Do I end up feeling like they're wrong or not good enough?

Merging and Distancing

1. Do I tend to feel badly about myself, as though my ideas and feelings aren't right or important, but then get angry if others don't listen or agree with me?

2. Do I try to please others, but when they aren't pleased get angry and shut down?

3. Do I tend to get very angry and walk away in a huff, but then feel guilty and try to make up to the person by being extra sweet or accommodating?

4. Do I let things slide to avoid conflict, but then blow up when I've just had enough already?

The Goal: Self-Differentiation

To be self-differentiated is a term from Bowen Family Systems, and it means to be connected to yourself with clear boundaries about your own thoughts and feelings, separate from those of others. You are self-attuned, which means you stay connected to yourself and your thoughts and feelings.

Self-differentiated means you can speak up about your thoughts, feelings and needs. You are emotionally honest, authentic and true to yourself. You stay securely attached to yourself and know your worthiness and value, and you don't get threatened, even if others disagree with or judge you.

At the same time, when you are self-differentiated you are curious about others and care about what is going on in them. You can listen openly to their feelings and needs without feeling threatened, triggering your defenses such as losing yourself, or judging them. You are able to stay in connection with others and securely attached to yourself.

Self-differentiation describes a vagal superstar. It's a brain that can stay in balance even in the most heated conversations. The goal is to be able to stay connected to yourself in these ways even when the conversation gets heated, tense, or awash in conflict—to feel your own feelings and needs, and to communicate your own thoughts and perspectives while at the same time staying present and connected with the other. It's a state which allows us to be connected to ourselves and the other at the same time. That's self-differentiation: not so self-focused that we are disconnected and not so other-focused that we are fused. It's a "both/and" state.

You can see how being self-differentiated means holding on to yourself.

MERGING
I lose my connection to myself.   DISTANCING
I lose my connection to you.

STAYING DIFFERENTIATED
I stay connected to myself and to you.

Boundary Tool for Self-Differentiation

Once you get a clear view of your tendencies, you can begin practicing the boundary tool.

Help with Merging Practice

If you tend to merge, take a deep breath and see if you can move your attention back to your own body and your own experience. How are you feeling? What are you needing? Maybe you notice that you tend to feel afraid, or worried, in tense conversations so you abandon your own needs and jump "over the boundary" to take care of the other person's needs.

Noticing without judging, reconnecting with your own feelings and needs, and staying attuned to yourself is the antidote to merging. As you practice noticing that your attention is "over there," and practice bringing it back "over here," your boundary thickens. The boundary is that safe space between you and the other person, your insulation.

Here are some of the core healthy beliefs that can go along with your practice. Remind yourself of these over and over again. They are beliefs that are absolutely true when you are in balance. It's only stress that separates you from them.

I can stay connected to my own feelings and needs.

I am present in my body.

I am listening to what is arising within me.

I can hear my own creative ideas.

I am connected to my heart, my higher intentions and values.

I can speak up when appropriate.

I can trust myself.

I can see and feel my inherent strength and worthiness.

I matter.

My thoughts, ideas, feelings and needs, matter.

Help with Distancing Practice

If you tend to distance when conflicts erupt, then practice taking a deep breath, and asking yourself "How is this person feeling right now? What might they need?" If you distance, you learned to create safety by cutting off from the other person and hiding behind a big thick wall of a boundary. Trying to connect with compassion and empathy with the other person will thin that wall down so you can stay present and connected.

Here are the core beliefs that can go along with your practice:

I can stay connected to the other person.

I can get a sense of their feelings and needs.

I can listen to them with an open mind and heart.

I can see their inherent strength and worthiness.

I can trust we can find a way through this together.

They matter.

Their thoughts, ideas, feelings and needs, matter.

Help with Both Merging and Distancing Practice

If you have a tendency to merge at some times, and distance at others, you will need to practice both of the above from time to time – depending on the person or situation.

How Does This All Fit Together?

In this chapter we discussed the foundation of how to hold on to yourself in tough conversations: strengthening habits which develop your vagal tone. We also looked at two fundamental relationship "safety valve" habits: merging and distancing. These are considered safety valves because they are our psychological system's attempt to keep us safe. As we mentioned, they are normal, but not necessarily healthy.

When you apply this concept to difficult conversations, merging tendencies might show up as people-pleasing, where you lose yourself and your message in an attempt to rescue or take care of others instead of being true to yourself. Giving in and abandoning yourself and your needs leads to an unhealthy stress state.

Distancing might show up as rejecting the other person, getting angry and belligerent, discounting or blaming/shaming the other, walking away or shutting down, ignoring their message, or dismissing them altogether with a cold shoulder.

You may also do a little bit of both. You may act passively accommodating or pleasing in front of the other, then aggressively discount them or complain to others about them behind their backs.

Holding on to yourself in tough conversations requires self-differentiation, the ability to stay securely attached and connected to yourself and to feel safety and security from within. In this state, no matter what is going on in the outer world, you can keep your vagal brake on and listen attentively, express yourself clearly, and come to healthy outcomes in conflicts.

CHAPTER 4

MINDFULNESS PRACTICES

"He who knows others is wise; he who knows himself is enlightened."

—*Lao Tzu*

The Key is Self-Awareness

Holding on to yourself requires self-awareness. Awareness allows you to observe, recognize, identify and understand your individual thumbprint of stress. Once you know what your triggers are, it will be easier to use tools to stay calm in any conversational storm.

As you strengthen self-awareness, you can catch yourself when you get triggered and help yourself move back to balance. You can take care of yourself when you are in the full blown stress response, so you won't further damage yourself, the relationship or what you are trying to communicate.

If you live the lifestyle most of us do, there will be times when you are not quite on top of it. You may be caught in heavy traffic. You might have a child who needs more attention. You might have a boss who's acting out his or her stress tendencies on you. You might simply be hungry or tired.

With a firmer foundation of self-awareness, you will have more options. You will notice more easily when you or another might be getting stressed. You will notice if you are merging or distancing, and can pull out your tools to create stronger self-differentiation in the moment.

It's our ability to bring our awareness to our inner states, our thoughts, feelings and stress level, to observe ourselves, that creates a critical tiny pause. This pause allows us to move from knee-jerk, hijacked reactions (that primitive bottom-up processing) to more thoughtful, balanced, top-down responses. This is the difference between reacting and responding. This inner pause of self-awareness is the threshold to change.

Prepare for Conflict

Just like exercise, it's best for our health to get in shape, and stay in shape, when it comes to preparing for conflict. If we can accept that conflict and stress are inevitable, we can choose to be prepared for their inevitable appearances. Dealing with conflict without strengthening our capacity to hold on to ourselves is like running a race without any training. You can do it, but chances are the results won't be to your liking.

How do you strengthen your ability to hold on to yourself?

It starts with practicing self-awareness. When you have stronger self-awareness skills you can bolster your ability to know and recognize your patterns, you can understand your stress levels and your tendencies, and you can create that tiny pause which will turn a potential blow up or melt down into a smoother, more balanced interaction.

Mindfulness—the Primary Tool For Building Self Awareness

Mindfulness is the simple (but not easy) practice of keeping, with intention, one part of your attention on your own inner state—your thoughts, feelings, body sensations, breathing and your stress state.

By intentionally keeping your attention anchored within, you are staying connected to yourself. It's easier to monitor your reactions, and to understand the other person in the moment. With mindfulness, you are harnessing the power of the mind to change the function and even structure of the brain.

One definition of mindfulness is the practice of bringing your attention to your experience in the present moment, non-judgmentally, with curiosity, openness, and acceptance.

When you are not practicing mindfulness, you go about your business lost in thought and habits, unaware of the present moment and what you are thinking, feeling or even doing. You can be lost in negative or judgmental thoughts about yourself, others, life and experience. This "lost in thought" means your default neural networks have taken over. You are on automatic pilot. This has been called "wandering mind" and is associated with higher degrees of depressed and anxious moods.

Practicing Mindfulness Changes the Structure and Function of Your Brain

Through a series of brain-oriented research in the last decade, scientists have discovered many valuable things about mental activity and the brain. Research on those who have meditated for a long time—and even on those who've only meditated for eight weeks—has shown distinct changes in brain structure and function.

Mindfulness practice helps thicken our cerebral cortex, the part of the brain involved in self-reflection and empathy.

Practicing mindfulness helps improve self-awareness and integrates our feelings and thoughts, improving how we handle stressful events.

Mindfulness practice was shown to help buffer against changes in the brain that can happen through aging.

Practicing mindfulness also has been shown to decrease density in the amygdala, meaning we are less easily provoked into fear, anger or threats in general. We are strengthening our capacity to be in a more balanced state more of the time and our capacity to hold on to ourselves even when outer circumstances are stressful.

Practicing mindfulness increases the left prefrontal cortex (PFC) dominance. Each of us tends to have either greater left PFC activity or greater right PFC activity. Studies have shown that people with more left-sided activation tend to be more approach oriented and emotionally positive, whereas people with more right-sided activation tend to be more avoidant/withdrawn and have more negative emotions such as anger, anxiety and depression. This difference is even present at birth and has been found to predict the length of time that it takes infants to cry after they are separated from the mothers. Mindfulness helps us shift to a more positive feeling and outlook.

A Taste of Mindfulness Practice

Let's practice mindfulness right in this moment. Practicing mindfulness at its essence is about training your focus. A common way to get started is to simply focus on one sensation, such as your breath, and the sensations created by a breath. As you sit reading this, see if you can focus on how the breath feels as it enters your nose, the coolness or the warmth of the breath or that tickling sensation right at your nostrils.

Just take a few breaths, and gently rest your attention on that spot, right where the air enters your nostrils. Feel the sensation of the breath moving in and then moving out of your nostrils. You are practicing mindfulness.

You can choose to focus on how the breath feels as it fills your body—the rise and fall, expansion and contraction of your belly area with your breath. Right now, see if you can softly place your attention, your focus, on the movement of your belly or chest area with your breath. Feel the sensation of that movement. As your attention wanders off from focusing on those sensations of the breath in your body (which it will do over and over again), gently, without judgment, bring your attention back to your breath.

Practice this for a few breaths and see how that feels. You are practicing mindfulness. You are paying attention to the present moment (the sensations in your body in this moment), on purpose and non-judgmentally, with an open and accepting mind.

Wheel of Awareness Practice

Daniel Siegel and others have described mindfulness in a way that can be useful to visualize. This description, called the "wheel of awareness," is something you can read to yourself from time to time, or draw as a visual. The wheel of awareness practice can strengthen your ability to operate from your center, from a balanced place. In this model the center of the wheel, the hub, is a place for you to become familiar with, so that you can go back to it when you start to feel triggered.

This hub of the wheel is a place to go to self-soothe and hold on to yourself. It is the state of being in balance or centered. It is located in the center of the wheel.

Imagine, or draw, a wheel with a hub at the center and spokes coming out from that hub. When you are present and aware, connected to the hub of the wheel, you are centered and balanced. You are aware of your inner experiences and what is streaming in through your senses. You can notice thoughts, feelings and body sensations.

It's that conscious awareness, that noticing and not merging into, (approach) or distancing away from (avoidance), that creates the space and pause that is good for your brain. When you are in the hub of the wheel, or balanced, you are connected to your body and to your inner self. This inner connection has been called many things, including your "sanctuary," your "wise self," your "essence" and your "spiritual connection or soul." It is where we experience a sense of wholeness and peace.

The spokes coming out from the hub represent where you can place, and sometimes lose, your attention and mental energies. One spoke can represent a mind focused on the past: remembering, ruminating, talking to imaginary others, saying what we wished we had said, going over what happened, or replaying memories and events.

Another spoke might be the mind jumping ahead to a focus on the future: planning, preparing, imagining, talking to yourself about a future event, making a mental list or worrying about something that might happen in the future.

A third spoke might lead to a place focused on yourself: obsessing about bodily sensations or your own feelings, thinking about what you want or don't want, grumbling about your life, who you are, how you are, and worrying and assessing if you are safe, worthy, loved, right or wrong, etc.

A fourth spoke can represent a mental focus on others: how do they feel? How do they view me? Are they better or worse than me? Are they right or wrong? Do I like and approve of me or not? Do I like or approve of them or not? What's wrong with them? How can I fix or change them? These are the mental patterns that play out as "merging" or "distancing" patterns of thought.

Being in the hub allows you to be aware when your attention travels down one of those spokes, but you can just as easily draw your attention back to the center. You are in balance and you don't lose the main focus: your center, your sanctuary, your core self.

Being out-of-balance means travelling down one or more of those spokes, or perhaps even camping out at one or more places and getting stuck there. Sometimes you may not even know you are habitually hanging out at one or more spots on the wheel.

Having a wheel of awareness practice allows you to check in with yourself about mental habits and helps you return to the hub—your center, your heart, your breath.

Keep in mind, this kind of activity is just what our minds are programmed to do—they jump about from past to future, self and others. Our thoughts tend to be regularly assessing worthiness, safety, health and status.

Fundamentally, like all mammals, our minds are assessing whether we should move toward something (attraction or approach) or away from something (aversion or avoidance). This is what our "default neural circuits" are up to—a constant stream of past, present, self, others, approach, avoidance. It is happening unconsciously or semi-consciously, and research suggests that the more we fall into a trance of believing these default circuits, following their ups and downs, the more easily we will move into stress states. We will be wired, tired, stressed and confused.

This is where mindful awareness comes in. By practicing mindful awareness, you are less vulnerable to stumbling into stress and you are less vulnerable to being triggered and caught off guard, falling into habitual reactions, or turning to bottom-up processing.

Labeling as a Mindfulness Practice

Several neurobiological studies have shown that when you use words to identify an emotion you are feeling, the prefrontal cortex becomes active and down-regulates the activity of the amygdala, the brain structure associated with negative feelings. So the mindfulness practice of noticing and labeling your feelings can serve to strengthen your capacity to hold on to yourself in tough conversations.

When you sit for a few minutes and notice how your feelings arise, and then label them "feeling" or "sadness," you are helping to downshift stress. This particular mindfulness practice is a powerful one, and it is best to do for a period of time until it feels natural and automatic. This is good preparation for noticing feelings when you get stressed in conversations.

Labeling (whether emotions, thoughts or bodily sensations) has been found to increase positive changes in the brain. For instance, if you find yourself focusing on an itch, a tension or a painful body sensation, you can just say "sensing" to yourself and bring your attention back to your breath. If you find yourself becoming aware of an emotion, you can say "feeling." If you find yourself lost in outside noises you can say "hearing." If you find yourself thinking, just say "thinking" softly to yourself and then bring your attention back to your breath. Always, gently bring your attention back to your breath.

This is a practice you can take into your waking life as well, not just "on the cushion." Even if you practice just a few mindful breaths throughout the day, you will be helping yourself unhook from negative habits and patterns. You will be strengthening the muscle that will help you stay cool in difficult conversations.

Deepening Our Understanding of Mindfulness

*"Mindfulness means paying attention in a particular way;
on purpose, in the present moment, and nonjudgmentally."*

This quote is from Jon Kabat-Zinn, a well-known teacher of mindfulness meditation and the founder of the Mindfulness-Based Stress Reduction program at the University of Massachusetts Medical Center.

Paying Attention "On Purpose"

When you practice mindfulness you consciously direct your attention, "on purpose." Just being aware that you are irritable or in a bad mood, or that you feel upset, is not necessarily being mindful.

If you are aware that you are irritable and want to practice mindfulness, you begin to focus on your breath and notice as thoughts, feelings and body sensations arise. You might notice where you feel the "irritable" feeling. You might notice your "irritable" thoughts as they come and go.

You purposely notice thoughts, feelings and sensations that arise for you as you gently bring your attention back to your breath. If the thought comes up, "Boy I am irritable" you can label that as "thinking." If you notice you are feeling frustrated or mad at yourself for being irritable, you can label that as "judging."

Another example is eating. You can be aware that you are eating. "Yes, I'm eating dinner." But eating mindfully will mean that as you eat, you are first aware of yourself breathing. You put your attention on your breath. Then you notice what body sensations arise. What do you taste? What does the texture of the food feel like in your mouth? If you suddenly find yourself thinking about someone or something, you simply notice it and bring your attention back to your breath, back to the body sensations as you eat.

Your mind might wander in all directions. Chances are much of this wandering is due to those default circuits and/or your salience network (the circuits in your brain that are checking for threats or dangers) at play. Just gently bring your attention back to your breath, and the sensations of eating. Perhaps you notice the scent of the food. "Smelling." Perhaps you notice sensations in your belly. "Sensing." Maybe you have a memory and some sadness comes to your attention. "Feeling."

When you're eating without mindful awareness you may be aware of what you're doing, but you're probably thinking about a hundred and one other things at the same time, and you may also be watching TV, talking, or reading—or even all three at once. So a very small part of your awareness is absorbed with eating, and you may be only barely aware of the physical sensations involved and even less aware of your thoughts and emotions.

Because you're only dimly aware of your thoughts, they wander in an unrestricted way. There's no conscious attempt to bring your attention back to your eating. There's no purposefulness. As mentioned earlier, this "wandering mind" has been implicated in fueling negative moods and stress.

Purposefulness is an important part of mindfulness. Having the purpose of staying with your experience means that you are actively shaping your mind. You're using your pre-frontal cortex, your "central executive network," and creating a more pronounced neural integration, which is key to brain health and development.

Paying Attention "In the Present Moment"

With mindfulness, you are tuning into what's arising in the present moment. When thoughts take you away from the present moment and you space out or get lost in thought, you simply try to notice this and just come back to the present.

Left to itself the mind wanders through all kinds of thoughts that are connected to all kinds of feelings—angry, disappointed, hopeless, helpless, self-pitying, grandiose, revengeful, bitter, joyous, self doubting—all kinds of thoughts and feelings come and go.

As we said earlier, most of these wandering, default thoughts and feelings tend to cluster around the past or present, or our selves or others.

If you are stuck in craving, addictions and bad habits, you might feel intense attraction or desire and your mind can narrow and over-focus on your craving. What food will you eat next? What do you need to buy or shop for? Your mind might over-focus on an addictive work project you are engaged in, or a relationship which you obsess over. Or let's say you over-focus on fixing yourself, or fixing someone else. There are many examples of a stuck "approach/attract" button, fueled by dopamine and our brain's reward system.

Mindful awareness helps us break through these addictive patterns of craving and desire by bringing your attention back to noticing what's going on right now. That doesn't mean you can no longer think about the past or future, or yourself and others, or even food and shopping, but when you do so, you do so mindfully. You're aware that right now you're thinking about the past or future, you are craving your substance, or you are focused on self or others.

This helps you create a pause, or a space in your habitual neural circuitry, and helps open up options for taking actions and responding. You are less likely to get hijacked and forced into unconscious patterns that aren't best for positive, balanced conversations.

By purposefully directing your awareness away from the busyness of your thoughts and towards the "anchor" of your breath and your body you decrease the effect that default neural circuits have on your life. You create that responsive pause that can take the place of a reactive upset, increasing your calm and cool in tough conversations.

Paying Attention "Non-Judgmentally"

When you practice mindfulness you're practicing noticing without judging, evaluating, or even reacting. You don't judge that this experience is good and that one is bad. Or if you do make those judgments, you simply notice that and let it go. If you are reacting, you are noticing it and letting those reactions rise and fall without clutching on to them.

When you practice mindfulness you are simply noticing and practicing accepting whatever arises. The tendency to wish things were different, to constrict yourself and resist your experience (which fuels the stress response) fades when you are practicing mindful awareness. Judging, resisting, getting upset at what you are noticing or experiencing creates what's called secondary stress. Secondary stress makes it more difficult to stay connected to yourself—balanced and able to listen in tough conversations.

Accepting and allowing the present moment to be as it is is one of the most important elements of mindfulness. Noticing, with acceptance. Releasing any resistance to what is. Whether it's a pleasant experience or a painful experience we treat it the same way.

This allowance of the moment is what Buddhists call equanimity. It helps us develop resilience to stress and retain our balance as conversations and life become difficult.

Experts Describe Mindfulness

David Rock: Founder and CEO of NeuroLeadership Group

"A study by Kirk Brown found that people high on a mindfulness scale were more aware of their unconscious processes. Additionally these people had more cognitive control, and a greater ability to shape what they do and what they say, than people lower on the mindfulness scale. If you're on the jetty in the breeze and you're someone with a good level or mindfulness, you are more likely to notice that you're missing a lovely day worrying about tonight's dinner, and focus your attention onto the warm sun instead. When you make this change in your attention, you change the functioning of your brain, and this can have a long-term impact on how your brain works too."

Daniel Seigel, M.D.: Clinical Professor of Psychiatry and Author, UCLA

"Mindfulness is defined as paying attention, in the present moment, on purpose, without grasping onto judgments. Mindful awareness has the quality of receptivity to whatever arises within the mind's eye, moment to moment. Recent studies of mindful awareness reveal that it can result in profound improvements in a range of physiological, mental, and interpersonal domains of our lives. Cardiac, endocrine, and immune functions are improved with mindful practices. Empathy, compassion, and interpersonal sensitivity seem to be improved. People who come to develop the capacity to pay attention in the present moment without grasping on to their inevitable judgments also develop a deeper sense of well-being and what can be considered a form of mental coherence."

Scott Bishop, PhD.: Clinical Psychology Professor and Author, University of Toronto

Dr. Bishop provides an "operation view" of mindfulness that has two components: "The first component involves the self-regulation of attention so that it is maintained on immediate experience, thereby allowing for increased recognition of mental events in the present moment. The second component involves adopting a particular orientation toward one's experiences in the present moment, an orientation that is characterized by curiosity, openness and acceptance."

More Mindfulness Tools

Centering Tool

This tool is one we recommend you begin to use throughout your day, several times a day if possible. If it's challenging to practice all the components, no problem, just choose one or two that are easy for you and doable. The point is the practice, not perfection. However, anything you practice is always good enough. It's the intention that matters most of all. Remember, it takes less than a minute to practice. The more you practice it, the more you can call on it in times of shifting states.

Staying connected to yourself means staying in your body, awake to the present moment and noticing what you are feeling, what your body sensations are telling you, and slowing down your "knee jerk" reactions or automatic thoughts and behaviors.

Here are the steps in the Centering Tool.

1. **Dignified Posture**

    Notice your posture. See if you can make any slight adjustments so you are in what Jon Kabat-Zinn calls the "dignified posture". Shoulders back, straighter spine, a slight smile. Give your brain the message that "all is well." You are using proprioception, helping the body communicate well-being and balance to the brain. A hunched or powerless posture won't help you activate your inner strength and balance.

2. Deep Breaths

Breathe into your belly, relaxing more with each exhale. This is the most important single practice you can do for your stress biology. Take as many belly breaths as you need to begin to feel a bit more present, a bit more relaxed. If you have a hard time belly breathing, clasp your hands behind your lower back and straighten your arms. This inhibits your chest muscles, making your diaphragm expand with your breath. This ensures belly breathing, and activates your parasympathetic nervous system, the antidote to the stress response. You can also practice elongating your exhale, which stimulates your parasympathetic nervous system. Breath in to the count of three, breathe out to the count of five.

3. Observe without Judgment

See if you can begin to observe yourself without judgment. Be curious about your feelings, sensations and thoughts. Warmly observe yourself in the present moment just as you are. Release any judgments or evaluations. Look at yourself as a loving parent might look upon a child. Or like a spiritual figure, a person or being that represents unconditional acceptance and love, might gaze upon you. Accepting, allowing, forgiving. Lovingly observe yourself; or at least observe yourself without judgment.

4. Bring Up a Feeling of Compassion or Kindness Toward Yourself

Take a moment to tune into your heart. See if you can practice feeling compassion or kindness toward yourself. You can use your inner voice. Say something kind or understanding to yourself in a tone of voice that is supportive and warm. Say words that help you feel better in this moment—words of empathy, appreciation and support, or words connecting you with your strength and courage and power.

Some people prefer to say a word that helps them feel balanced, whole and connected. Words like peace, love, om, shalom, God, thank you, are all examples of commonly used words to help center and balance oneself.

Practice these four steps on their own, in combination or all together. In any combination, these steps create a pause to bring yourself back to a balanced state.

Sense Based Mindfulness Tool

You can practice sense-based mindfulness. Even 30 seconds throughout the day will help. Labeling calms the stress response and helps with neural integration, so labeling your senses helps you decrease stress. If you are in the heat of the moment and are starting to get triggered, use this mindfulness practice to bring yourself back into balance.

- Tune in to one of your senses.
- Listen to the sounds within the room, outside of the room.
- Say to yourself, "listening" or "hearing."
- Feel the air against your skin, the texture of your pants against your legs, the feeling of the ground beneath your feet.
- Say, "sensing."
- Taste the food that you are eating. Taste each bite, each flavor, each texture.
- Say to yourself, "tasting."
- As your attention naturally moves, notice it and label the direct experience "feeling," "hearing," and "sensing."

Emotion Based Mindfulness Tool

Since labeling calms the stress response and helps with neural integration, you can also practice labeling your feelings as a mindfulness practice. Again, any length of a check-in is useful—even 30 seconds throughout the day will help. With this practice, you simply take a breath or two and ask yourself: "What am I feeling right now?" Wait for one or two breaths to see what response arises. Think of the basic feelings: angry, sad, afraid, guilty, tired, lonely, grateful, peaceful, happy, secure, rested, loved, or loving.

Labeling Needs Mindfulness Tool

To balance the tendency to merge or lose touch with yourself, you can sit quietly and mindfully, and ask yourself: "What am I needing right now?"

The answer may be simply to pause and breathe. Or maybe you need something practical like water, a restroom, or to close your eyes for a moment to rest. When you become aware of a need, it's important to follow through, even if it's only for a few seconds. You build your trust in yourself this way, and your strength in self-regulation.

All these practices can come in handy for when you really need them: when you are triggered.

More Practice, Less Triggered

These mindfulness tools can serve as inoculations against the stress response and help ease the pain of getting triggered by difficult conversations. As you practice during more neutral moments, you are building your mindfulness muscle.

You'll be stronger and more able to stay present and connected as stress mounts. You will be less reactive, so your brain's natural drive to go into fight/flight/freeze/submit mode will be eased.

Practicing mindfulness will provide you with a solid foundation of self-awareness. You will be able to prevent or ease the pain of disconnection and misunderstanding that happens when you go out-of-balance in important conversations.

Mindfulness sets the stage for greater resilience during tough times. It is our foundation. Being human, we will all still get triggered, and particularly challenging people, situations and topics will send us into the stress response. However, having a strong foundation will help you face those moments of conflict and stress more adaptively. Cultivating a mindful awareness practice is the foundation for being able to stay present in difficult conversations.

These mindfulness tools also help when you are triggered. The next few chapters will introduce other tools to use once you've been triggered into stress. Start by practicing mini-moments of mindfulness as you continue to read through these chapters.

CHAPTER 5

USE MINDFULNESS TO IDENTIFY YOUR STRESS STATES

"The range of what we think and do is limited by what we fail to notice. And because we fail to notice that we fail to notice there is little we can do to change until we notice how failing to notice shapes our thoughts and deeds."
—*R.D. Laing*

Now that we've outlined the importance of practicing mindfulness, and you've had a little practice with some basic mindfulness tools, let's apply this to becoming more aware of your stress states.

Becoming more mindful of your own stress state is a vital tool in knowing whether you should believe your thoughts or challenge them, as well as helping you decide what tools to use and how to support yourself through any difficulty that arises.

As we outlined earlier, we've simplified our internal stress response into three basic states.

Quick Review: Three States

1. **Balanced.** In this inner state, you are in homeostasis and all systems are humming along, integrated and balanced. You can speak openly

and with compassion. You are connected to yourself and the other person. You feel free to share your feelings and needs, and you listen to the other person's perspective with understanding. The communication stays more relaxed and open. In general you feel secure, worthy, capable, balanced and present.

Your brain is in top-down processing mode and your vagal brake is on. You feel safe and connected.

2. **Triggered.** In this inner state, your stress hormones and schemas are beginning to get activated. You may begin to doubt yourself or to have feelings like worry, fear, anger or guilt. You may begin to edit your conversation and not feel safe. It's harder to listen to the other person. You may find yourself beginning to judge them or defend yourself. You perceive the hints of a threat (to your identity, self esteem, point of view, security, or even your life) and your body and conditioning are beginning to take over. You are moving toward your unconscious, fight/flight/freeze/submit posture.

    You are on the edge and starting to slip away from that calm, cool, collected person you like to be.

3. **Out-of-balance.** Here your stress hormones and neurobiology have hi-jacked your balance and you are diving down into a more primitive brain state. Your feelings are ramped up or shut down completely. You can no longer really hear what another is saying. You've forgotten your message and have gotten caught in past memory loops or schemas. Your anger or panic, self-doubt or anxiety are in full swing. Your thinking has become all-or-nothing, black-and-white, tunnel-focused, negative, judging or rigid. You are in full-blown stress mode. Your fight/flight/freeze/submit response is fully activated.

    Your brain is in bottom-up processing and your vagal brake is off, meaning you have little control over what you do, say, think or feel. You are disconnected from yourself and from the other person.

Reflect on Your Own Experiences of the Stress States

Take a moment to reflect on how you tend to think, feel and respond when you are in these three states. As we said earlier, early trauma or difficulties can prime the brain to go more easily into stress, and your brain can get stuck in stress, coloring your experience, responses and perceptions.

It can be valuable to note if you tend to get stuck in triggered or out-of-balance states at home, at work, or both. It can also help to notice if others in your life tend to spend more time triggered or out-of-balance.

Limbic Resonance

The good news is that the tools we present will help you move back to more moments of homeostasis or balance. As you raise your brain out of stress, those around you will benefit as their brain state will tend to rise too. This is due to "limbic resonance." Limbic resonance is the tendency for our emotional energy to impact those around us. The more we can strengthen our connection to ourselves, the stronger we can impact the emotions of those around us. We've all known people who just seem calm. They carry that presence with them. How do you feel when you are around them? That's limbic resonance!

Of course it works the other way too. Think about someone who tends to be grouchy, negative, irritable or discounting. How do you tend to feel around them? We have that kind of impact on each other—a kind of emotional contagion. We can catch each other's emotions.

What is Your Unique Stress Thumbprint?

Applying mindfulness to your stress response means spending time reflecting on how your tendencies under stress play out for you personally. Each stress thumbprint is different, and knowing your own gives you more feedback information for when you are starting to get out-of-balance.

Take a moment to reflect on how you tend to think, feel and respond when you are in these three states. Think of a difficult situation, relationship or conversation you've experienced lately. This could be either at home or at work—whatever comes to mind and seems to hold a bit of an emotional charge in the recalling.

Imagine what happens for you as your stress gets triggered. Now, create three columns on a piece of paper. In the left column write "Thoughts." In the middle column write "Feelings" and in the right column, write "Behaviors."

You can create a few columns on a piece of paper that would look like this:

Triggered

Thoughts	Feelings	Behaviors

Out-of-Balance

Thoughts	Feelings	Behaviors

Balanced

Thoughts	Feelings	Behaviors

Now jot down some of the cues that can help you identify your stress state.

Try to notice....

1) What are your unique signs of being triggered? What thoughts do you think in a triggered state that are clues that you might

be getting stressed? What are the feelings you experience in your body? What are the behaviors? It is especially important to raise your awareness about your triggered state, as this is the state where you have the highest chances of circumventing the full blown stress response and avoiding conversation disasters. Think about something that recently irritated you—at home or at work. Not an incident where you "lost it," but one that was just irritating. What do you often say about the other person or yourself or the situation? What do you often feel? What do you often do? Capture these in the three columns.

2) Now, reflect on what happens when you go into that full-blown stress response. What do you notice about what you are thinking? Are there some familiar thoughts? Familiar feelings? Typical behaviors? Learn to recognize yourself as you slip into this state. Also, practice some self-forgiveness about these times. Once we slip into a full-blown stress response, it's often too late to do much but some basic damage control to extricate ourselves before more damage is done. The power and leverage in this state happens by raising our awareness—either preventing the state, or minimizing the damage it can cause. Go back to the three columns, and capture your full-blown stress state thoughts, feelings and behaviours in the three columns.

3) Lastly, consider when you are in "Balance." What are you thinking? Feeling? What are your behaviors and actions like? See if you can remember and highlight the conversations and moments when you felt in balance and stayed in balance, even when the going got tough. We're going to help you strengthen and increase these times so it's good to know where you are heading!

Just by beginning to notice these patterns you are increasing your self-awareness and laying down the foundation for change. Can you build in a practice where you are simply asking yourself daily: "What state am I in?" You can do this a few times a day: at the start of your day, at your mid-morning coffee break, at lunch, at the afternoon break, and before heading into dinner. You can even enlist others at work to help remind each other:

"What state are you in?" Setting a timer or putting it in your computer or calendar are also other ways to support your practice.

Increasing mindful awareness of your stress states strengthens your ability to hold onto yourself through stressful conversations and situations.

Maybe you found it challenging to jot down how your stress state is impacting you. No problem. Just start noticing...what are your signs of being triggered? What happens when you go into the full blown stress response? What situations trigger you? What people? Beginning to notice these patterns increases your self-awareness and your resilience when the time comes to manage your stress response.

Here are some more questions to reflect upon as you grow in your self-awareness of your triggers and full-blown stress.

1. What relationships or people tend to push your buttons? Who do you find yourself reacting negatively to? List the people in your work and family or social life that trigger you.
2. Are there particular situations at work that tend to trigger you? Please list them here.
3. Do you find some requests or topics particularly difficult to bring up? List your "tough-to-talk-about" topics.

Your answers to these questions will give you opportunities to practice your new tools and skills in staying balanced, connected and calm in conflicts and stress.

Emotional Memory Makes it More Difficult

We get triggered when we feel threatened. That seems clear enough. But what makes this whole system more challenging is that often we don't even realize we are triggered or that we feel threatened. This is all happening sub-cortically, meaning below our conscious awareness. The slight raise of an eyebrow or the tiny shift in vocal tone can trigger our stress response. We don't know what hit us.

What triggers you and what triggers me may be vastly different due to our emotional histories. Each of us has experiences when we are young that give us information about ourselves and the world around us. Our brains soak in all the stimuli from the environment but it is stimuli with a strong emotional component that is most likely to "stick" in our neural circuitry. The unconscious structures in our brain strive to remember experiences with strong emotions attached. Any slight suggestion of similar emotional material, or a stimulus in the environment that reminds us of these past events, can trigger us into a stress reaction—fight, flight, freeze or submit.

These have been called "schemas," emotional memories from the past that get replayed in the present. We'll be taking a closer look at this in the next chapter. Once again, the adage "It's not me, it's my wiring" applies. When we get triggered it is often the vestiges of unconscious memories that are at play. As you strengthen your emotional base, you'll be less apt to fall into these unconscious patterns, and more able to compassionately support yourself when you do.

CHAPTER 6

STRESSFUL CONVERSATIONS ARE CLOUDY MIRRORS --SCHEMAS

"We don't see things as they are. We see things as we are."
—Anais Nin

"The mind in its natural state can be compared to the sky, covered by layers of cloud which hide its true nature."
—Kalu Rinpoche

When we find ourselves in difficult conversations and begin to get triggered into the stress response, our brain structures, hormones and neurochemicals will slam us into early emotional memories against our will. These early memories were downloaded during emotion-filled stressful times imprinted in our brain from our past. The stronger the emotion, the more impactful the early memory will be, and the more influential this memory will be on current situations.

That's why stressful conversations are, ultimately, about you and your memories. The severity of the reaction speaks to something within you that is coming alive. It's not a rationale choice. It also explains why stressful conversations are called our "buddhas on the path." They are an opportunity to stretch and grow beyond where you are at the moment. These high-trigger moments bump you into the areas where you are in most need of growth, relearning and change. But that's also why they feel so threatening, upsetting and scary. In AA they are called AFGOs (Another F*^# Growth Opportunity).

Schemas

Schemas are waves or patterns of sensation, thought, feeling and belief that become encoded in our neural circuits based on early learning. Schemas can easily be false associations false assumptions and expectations, and false beliefs. However, when we are in stressed states, our body and brain often feel and act as if the schemas were true.

If you have had powerful moments of feeling unloved, not good enough or unworthy in your past, and just about all of us have, these feelings can be re-triggered instantly in stressful conversations. If you tended to feel angry or victimized as a child, this same feeling may get activated in your current conversations. No matter how strong, smart or healthy you might be, old emotional memories can get triggered in present day experiences. These memories do not need to match the reality of what is going on in the present moment. They only need to vaguely resemble a past emotional memory.

To complicate matters, these memories are stored in your unconscious, implicit memory, and you can be completely unaware of them. But it doesn't take much to bring them forward—a scent from that time period, someone who's tone of voice might be similar to that of someone you didn't like, a raise of an eyebrow.

It's your schemas that can send you from balanced to a full-blown stress response. Your schemas interrupt the flow of two-way, productive conversation, and derail your attempts to get your point across, express yourself, advocate for yourself, or listen to another.

Remember that this all happens in an unconscious or semi-conscious way. It might just be a vague sensation or it could be an abrupt, intense reaction that is schema-driven. You may not know exactly how you feel or what's going on in the moment. All you know is that you're upset. Or angry. Or reactive. Schemas are challenging to re-wire because they are so hidden. But now you will have the understanding and the tools to alter these basic patterns.

Schemas as Opportunities

Schemas are common belief patterns that get internalized when we are young and impressionable.

No matter how healthy and normal an upbringing you had, we are all vulnerable to unconscious schemas being downloaded in childhood. When we are little, our brains are not fully developed and are rapidly making connections. However, we are unable to see the big picture or to truly understand a larger context for our experiences. We have stressful moments where it feels like our basic human needs aren't or can't be met. These are moments of panic, shame or rage, and faulty beliefs and expectations can be downloaded and then encoded into our survival wiring.

In stress and conflict, most of us have one or more resident schemas that get activated and throw us into disconnected, full blown stress. Raising awareness about our own schemas gives us more opportunities to heal old wounds, rewire faulty beliefs and be more present and balanced in conflict and tough conversations.

It's Not You, It's Not Them, It's Your Wiring (And Probably Theirs Too!)

When you are cruising along in life, in a balanced state, these schemas are far beneath the surface of your thoughts and you can feel powerful, worthy, and connected to others. Wonderful! But when stress mounts, or when you feel threatened in any way, your survival wiring is activated, you get triggered or go into the full blown stress response, and these early schemas start rearing their fear-based, uncomfortable heads.

Feeling threatened doesn't have to have any logic to it. Any of us can feel threatened easily, especially if there is a schema involved. Just like a dog that starts to growl and bark if it feels it's backed in a corner, we too have similar primitive survival mechanisms that can override our best intentions or usual temperaments. In fact, an early encounter with a barking dog may be triggered by a loud conversation with a bellicose boss!

Stressful conversations are particularly challenging to navigate as not only are your schemas getting activated, chances are pretty high that the other person's schemas are getting triggered too. We can fall into anger and blame, we can ridicule, criticize, and shame ourselves and the other person, but that just adds gas to the flame. It's no one's fault. There's not a winner and loser, it's your stress biology taking over. Time to let go of the criticism and blame, and begin to rewire your own schemas.

Basic Human Needs and Schemas

Here are some basic human needs we all share and some common schemas that are often linked to each. See if any of these schemas sound familiar to you. We have italicized the thoughts or beliefs that you may experience when a schema has been triggered. No worries if you recognize yourself in each of these schemas, as that is normal. All are simply the memory of unmet needs.

Basic Human Needs	Schemas That Can Be Downloaded
Love & Connection	Abandonment. *I'll be rejected. I don't belong. I am alone or will be left all alone. I am not loveable. They don't like me.* Feeling: Fear, anxiety, worry Sensations: Closing in, panic, hard to breath, tightening in throat
	Mistrust. *I'm vulnerable to harm. It's not safe. I can't trust others. I can't trust life, myself, the universe. They are lying. Something bad is going to happen.* Feeling: Doubt, anger, fear Sensations: Alert, narrowing of eyes, holding your breath, ready to flee

	People-Pleasing/Merging. *My needs don't matter, only yours do. I need you to be okay for me to be okay. I need you to approve of me to be worthy. Oh no. I've made them mad. It's not okay to upset them.* Feeling: Fear, worry, appeasement Sensations: Panic, fast breathing, anxious movements, jumping in to make it better
Power & Agency	Helplessness/Powerlessness. *I can't meet my needs and my needs don't matter. I'm dependent. Incompetent. Nothing works out for me. I might as well give up. Nothing I do matters. This will never change.* Feeling: Depressed. Sunken. Alone. Lost Sensations: Collapsing in, loss of energy, eyes down, heavy heart
	Hypercritical/Distancing. *I need to be perfect to be OK and so do they. I am never good enough and neither are others. I am critical of self, others, life. They can't get it right. They are all wrong. Or I can't get it right. I am all wrong.* Feeling: Anger, rage, resentment, frustration Sensations: Tight fists, rapid heart rate, busy mind, storming away
	Controlling. *I need to control the situation and you to be safe. I have to have complete control and have all the power. This is ridiculous. How dare they. Why can't they see? They are a fool.* Feeling: Anger, frustration, fury Sensations: Chest pounding, clenched fists, stomping around, slamming doors

Recognition & Worthiness	Self-Blame. *I am bad. It must be my fault. I am to blame. I'm a failure. I'm no good. It's all my fault. I screwed up. I'm the worst. There's something wrong with me.* Feeling: Shame, guilt, anxiety, sadness Sensations: Hollow chest, heavy heart, eyes look down, tears
	Worthiness. *I am not good enough. I don't deserve. I'm not worthy. I can't make a difference/my contributions don't matter.* *I am not OK. There's something wrong with me. I am no good. I have no value in this. I am wrong.* Feeling: Sadness, depression, loneliness Sensations: Collapsing shoulders, head lowered, numbness

When in stress, our thoughts tend to become rigid, negative and tunnel-visioned. These thoughts, with enough emotional energy or repeated over time, can become our core faulty beliefs. Come across a painful, familiar feeling and most likely it is attached to one of these familiar beliefs.

If you are in stress often or fall into a chronic stress state you can begin to operate habitually from these old schemas.

Raising Schema Awareness in Conflict

As you were reading through the chart on typical schemas above, did any jump out at you as familiar? Did you notice your breath catch, your heart jump, or stomach clench? Even subtly? Chances are, any that grabbed your attention or created a body response may be important to your own emotional history and wiring.

Remember, these schemas are universal, so there is no judgment or blame necessary; this is just the human condition, what we all face as a species trying to survive and thrive in the world.

Questions to Increase Your Schema Awareness

Bring to mind a conflict, chronic issue or stressful relationship. Now consider your feelings, thoughts and behaviors during this recall.

1. How do I feel when I think about this stressful situation or conflict with someone? Do I get angry and resentful? Feel shame or powerlessness? Begin to feel anxious and afraid?

    Feelings give you clues to your schemas.

2. What kinds of repetitive thoughts stream through my mind when I'm triggered? Do I go into blaming and hateful thoughts? Thoughts about my own weaknesses and failures? Thoughts about how unfair life is or how I never get what I want?

    Your thoughts will also give you clues about your schemas.

3. What do I notice in my body? Do I make fists and move toward the person? Do I recoil and sink into myself? Do I turn away or look down to avoid eye contact? Do my eyes get large and intense as I stare down at the person? Does my stomach clench and my throat tighten?

    Body sensations also give clues to schemas.

As you start to notice more of what you are feeling, thinking and sensing, go back to the list of schemas and see what looks familiar now.

Another Way of Looking at Basic Human Needs: SCARF

If the three basic needs outlined above didn't quite fit for you, here's another model to consider. This model can be helpful in organizational or business settings, and comes from David Rock's book, *Your Brain at Work*. Rock describes five fundamental social mammalian needs that, if we perceive are threatened, can throw us into the stress response.

The acronym Rock uses to capture these five basic human needs is **SCARF.**

S = Status. We feel a threat to our status in our group, family or team. Status equals security to social mammals.

C = Certainty. The human brain loves certainty. It loves to predict and control. Why? Prediction and control feels safer, more secure.

A = Autonomy. We thrive when we feel we are self-determining and free. If our freedom and autonomy feels threatened, it feels like our survival is at risk.

R = Relatedness. We are social and thrive in community. If our sense of belonging and relatedness (being valued in relationship) feels threatened, our survival needs will feel threatened.

F = Fairness. When our sense of fairness or our values feel at risk, we feel our safety is at risk.

Just like the three needs stated earlier, when we feel like these basic mammalian needs are not being met, we get triggered, lose connection with ourselves, and the stress response is activated. Our thoughts, feelings and behaviors become obstacles to having effective, rewarding conversations. It's the stress response itself and what it does to our internal processing that will continue to give us that experience that our basic human needs are not getting met. It becomes a self-fulfilling prophecy.

Another Way of Looking at our Basic Human Experience: Malas

David Rock has identified the five basic human needs from a neuroscience and social science point of view. An ancient system for identifying schemas can be found in a model called the Malas, taken from the yogic and Hindu traditions. It's simple, yet can have a much broader context.

The three malas are three "veils," or myths that prevent us from seeing our true nature or our true selves. The yogic philosophy teaches that when we are brought into this world, we don these veils and wear them throughout our lives.

Parts of these three malas reside in each of us. See which veils, or faulty belief patterns, might be obscuring your view of your true self.

Anava Mala—Unworthiness

The first veil is called the Anava mala, or the myth of unworthiness. Tara Brach, in her book, *Radical Acceptance*, calls this the "trance of unworthiness." Anava mala is the veil that disconnects us from our core worthiness and wholeness, resulting in low self-esteem, insecurity, and a worried preoccupation with self. We end up feeling not good enough or broken, needing to be fixed, less than others, or ashamed of who we are.

When you are trapped under the Anava mala, you forget your true nature and become blind to your goodness, wisdom and strength. You may develop a sense of isolation and loneliness, and an over-focus on what is wrong with you or your problems and faults. It's easy to get stuck on the non-stop wheel of trying to fix and change yourself.

We all are vulnerable to fall under this "veil of unworthiness," and it shows up in many areas of our lives. It can get triggered in an instant, and leave us feeling badly about ourselves, stuck in our flaws and weaknesses, disconnected from our value, worth and strengths.

Difficult conversations can easily activate this mala. Feeling less-than, unworthy, of little value, not heard or understood, powerless, or not good enough can all be signs of this mala showing up in your communications.

The antidote to this mala is to cherish, connect with, and trust your true self: your essential self, your divine nature. The antidote requires accepting that you are human, that you make mistakes and have weaknesses.

You can bring to conversations your essential worthiness, but also your vulnerability—knowing you aren't perfect (and neither are they) but also knowing you don't have to be (and neither do they).

Accepting you aren't perfect and that you have a dark side or a "shadow" is important to lifting this veil. You don't have to be perfect to be worthy.

You don't have to be anything other than who you are. There is nothing to fix or change. You were born worthy, and you retain that essential worthiness throughout your life span.

Maiya Mala—Separation

The second mala, the Maiya mala, is the myth of separation. This second veil leads us to believe we are separate from others and from all of life, separate from nature and from the spiritual. We can suffer in aloneness, feelings of not belonging, negative comparisons, and isolation when this mala is triggered.

When you are trapped under the Maiya mala, you can get lost in comparing yourself with others and in your self-judgment or judgment of others. Your mind is busy judging and comparing—am I better-than or worse-than? Is she, he or it better-than or worse-than? Over and over your mind can be judging and evaluating, checking to see who is coming out on top, who is on bottom. You can lose your sense of connectivity, or shared strength and mutual intentions. It doesn't feel safe to be vulnerable and connected. It's easy to lose your sense of humanity and the oneness of all life. You can lose your sense of the sacred.

This mala shows up in difficult conversations when you feel angry and hateful, or try to push away, distance from and reject the other person. Or, you may end up feeling alone, like no one understands you, and like you can't connect with or understand the other person.

The antidote to this mala is to embrace your vulnerability, be open, authentic, and alive. Feel your true feelings, acknowledge your strengths and weaknesses and lovingly accept the strengths and weaknesses of others. See all as a reflection of the one, and the one as a reflection in all.

In conversation, you can sense that it is you, a part of the great oneness of all, communicating with the other, who also represents the great oneness.

Remembering where we came from and where we are going can also help. We are made from the same molecules and energy systems that are a part of all of life. We breathe in and out, sharing the same oxygen with every living thing around us. We share energy and atoms with each person we encounter. Life is an ecosystem, and we are a fundamental part of the flow.

Karma Mala—Doingness

The third veil is the Karma mala, the myth of "doingness." This myth tells us that there is something we need to do in order to be OK. We get stuck in performing, proving ourselves, or operating on "shoulds" to impress or feel safe with others. We think our value comes from our accomplishments, or we fall into the pattern of feeling not accomplished enough, like what we do is not good enough or not right.

The myth of doing will fuel over-thinking and "trying, trying, trying." It will fuel overworking, overeating, anxieties, compulsions and obsessions. We can get stuck in trying to figure things out, spinning our wheels and falling into this "busy busy" behavior. This mala makes it easy to become trapped in perfectionism and overworking.

Our marketing and media set the bar so high, we can never really reach it. We can get stuck working to fix, change, or make things and ourselves better, but we end up with a sense of failure and inadequacy. Or we become overwhelmed with all that we have to accomplish and feel fearful, powerless and anxious.

In conflict or difficult conversations, this mala can send you into an anxious drive to *fix it* or solve the problem. It's easy to then ramp up into over-responsibility, thinking you need to do something, when often just listening and making space for differing opinions is all that is needed. But this mala can slam you into a desperate need to take action.

The antidote to this mala is to trust in your essence, that deepest quality of your being. It takes a trust in the inherent purposefulness of life, there is no desperate rush to a finish line. There's not always an urgency toward an answer or an action. Doing can be helpful, fun and creative. Accomplishments can feel good. But it is the quality of being that you bring to your doing that matters most. It is not about what you do, but the spirit and energy, the intention behind it. You can remind yourself over and over to enter into the deep, true, loving essence that you are. And that is enough.

In conversation, you can practice relaxing and letting the communication unfold, with curiosity and awareness, rather than an urgent need for outcome and achievement.

You can move back to your heart, your deeper values and intentions, and slow down on the doing so that each action has more meaning. You can focus on how you want to be in the world, what qualities and energy you want to contribute, and let go of some of the over focus on mindless or less intentional doing.

The First Step in Re-Wiring is Awareness and Compassion

Each of these models give us clues to what might get triggered in difficult conversations, throwing us into our survival circuitry and the stress response. You know by now the foundation is self-awareness. So simply noticing what tends to arise for you is useful—which of the schemas are most reflected in your experience, if there are SCARF needs that are trigger points for you, or when the malas might color your experience.

The first step in re-wiring your stress-related tendencies is always self-awareness and compassion. You have begun to set the stage for change if you can have empathy and understanding for your own humanity; for that which arises in your inner life, not by choice necessarily but by conditioning. When you can practice observing it and limiting your judgment, analysis, criticism and self-condemnation, you will be firmly upon the first step.

From Awareness to Action

Now you've been introduced to the basic foundation for how to hold on to yourself: strengthening your self-awareness, building mindfulness and understanding your triggered schemas. The next few chapters will introduce tools and practices that you can use to build your stress resilience and move you in the direction of re-wiring your early brain conditioning and schemas. By practicing these tools you will find yourself triggered less frequently and less intensely. Please remember you don't have to do any of this perfectly, or even well. Good enough, as best you can, and "just a beginner" is perfect. The exciting work starts now!

CHAPTER 7

TOOLS TO USE WHEN YOU ARE TRIGGERED

"Every problem has a gift for you in its hands."
—*Richard Bach*

By now, you are familiar with the three kinds of brain states, the importance of mindfulness, and why conflict hits us so hard. We are often triggered by schemas or perceived threats from long ago that have very little to do with the present situation. We may have underlying needs that in our perception are not being met. We may very well be living out of our own painful memories, old survival wires activated, as we lose our ability to listen, understand, and creatively problem-solve.

Building a foundation of mindfulness skills gives you the ability to notice when your brain state is moving from a balanced place to a triggered one. You will need mindfulness as a go-to skill when you are triggered.

This chapter focuses on tools you can use when you enter into a threat-signaling state—that is, when triggered. In the triggered state, you are still present enough to notice and gather inner resources to move back to balance and connection. You haven't been slammed into the full-blown stress response, where it becomes nearly impossible to salvage the moment and return to your wise and compassionate self. You may be able to use a tool in the moment to calm yourself down, but often times you will find yourself walking away from the situation wondering what happened. That is also the right time to use one of the tools from this chapter.

Getting Triggered is a Point of Choice

Knowing what to do when you find yourself triggered is important because this is the state of choosing. Depending on how much mindful self-awareness you've cultivated as part of your daily life, you will have varying degrees of capacity to realize when you are headed into this state. The more you work on your mindfulness skills, the more choice you will have when triggered.

This chapter will present three types of tools for you to try out.

The first type of tool is a powerful one to use at a deeper level, and we call it a "Schema Reframe Tool." One of the gifts of being triggered is that it gives you an opportunity to notice and reframe early learning patterns, the faulty beliefs that throw you out-of-balance. As we discussed in the last chapter, much of conflict is really about us, not the other person. So taking the time to do the work of a schema reframe helps to sort out what's yours and what isn't.

The second type of tool we've included is a selection of three strategies to cultivate more curiosity when you are getting triggered, since curiosity is such a powerful antidote to the narrowing of focus that happens with stress.

The third type of tool is a selection of three strategies to use right in the moment to calm and soothe your triggered brain. We've got one adapted from the Heart Math Institute which has some strong science behind it for shifting your brain state and heart/brain coherence, moving you back to a balanced state significantly and quickly. We have also included a loving kindness tool, as well as a tool that's been called a "Hawaiian practice" as a guide.

Schema Reframe Tool

The Schema Reframe Tool is a powerful one to help you whenever you've become triggered, or find yourself in conversational loops in important relationships. This is a transformational tool, so use it often and you will find yourself better and better able to stay connected with yourself and in balance, regardless of the topic, situation or person you are with.

This tool is not one that you would use in the moment. Rather, use this tool after you have been triggered, and have gotten some distance from the person or situation but can still feel your upset feelings.

The key to making this tool work is to really feel your feelings. Emotions open up core memory circuits deep in your brain. Look at feelings as an opportunity to open up awareness and to embrace the possibility for growth and change.

When the situation brings up primitive, strong, out-of-balance feelings, you have an opportunity to witness core faulty belief patterns or schemas. It is very powerful to catch a glimpse of what those original schemas are while they are in action; seeing them get activated gives you the opportunity to rewire old communication habits.

This particular tool is something we've adapted from Emotional Brain Training (EBT). EBT was developed over the last 30 years by Laurel Mellin, PhD, in collaboration with scientists and university-based researchers. EBT is a science-based program teaching the skills of self-regulation and integrating advances in neuroscience and stress physiology. The tool is useful when we are triggered but are not really sure what's beneath it all.

Even though the stress that arises from difficult conversations seems perfectly justified, it usually is caused by an old memory, as we've outlined in previous chapters. That old memory is a wire encoding a basic expectation or schema about life that is not reasonable. It was wired when you were in stress early in life, and gets retriggered when you are in stress now.

The Format of the Schema Reframe Tool

You can use this tool on your own, simply by reading out the question prompts and thinking about your answers. A more powerful way to use this tool, however, is as a journaling exercise. You can set aside 20 to 30 minutes to ask yourself the following and journal your responses. This tool can also be used with someone asking you the questions and being a supportive listener for you (no fixing, just a compassionate presence).

Step 1. Ask yourself: What's going on?
Just a few sentences describing the facts of the situation.

Step 2. Feel your feelings.

I feel angry…

I feel sad…

I feel afraid…

I feel guilty…

Stick to the four most basic feelings and express them, even if only to yourself. Emotions are primitive and messy. Don't try to sound nice or good. Get low, messy and real here! Express the feelings that are the hardest to own up to! One key: allow all of your feelings…make space for them… they are just feelings, energies in your body, and are designed to arise, be felt and cared for, and resolved. The more you allow all of your feelings to be OK and give them space and room in your experience, the easier they will pass and help you move forward.

Step 3. Find your unreasonable expectation.

My unreasonable expectation:

Pause, it may take a while to see it. Look for "shoulds" or "should nots" about yourself, others or life. Look for black-and-white thinking. Look for negative predictions or untrue judgments. Look for schemas.

Step 4. Turn it around to become a reasonable expectation and repeat.

Take your unreasonable expectation and turn it around into a more reasonable one.

This is usually the opposite of the unreasonable belief you uncovered in the previous step. Choose something that feels good and true in your body as you say it. Repeat it a few times. If the words evolve, that's fine. You are looking for a shift in your perspective, feelings, or understanding. You are looking to connect with your deeper wisdom and truth here. Don't worry if it sounds hollow or untrue at first. Over time as you practice feeling the feelings that arise, noticing with mindfulness, staying in your body and with your breath instead of running to the fight/flight/freeze/submit response, your old wires will begin to rewire to the new, transformative statement that aligns with your wise self and heart.

Step 5. Look for the deeper pattern that might be getting triggered.

Perhaps this upset is triggered by a schema, mala or faulty belief laid down early in life. Find the schema or mala and see if you can find a more adaptive, life-supporting belief that is it's opposite.

Repeat this new belief over and over, especially when you are exercising or in a relaxed or meditative state. Keep repeating the meaningful phrases throughout the day.

An Example of the Schema Reframe Tool in Action

Let's examine an example to show you how the tool works in action. Let's suppose someone we'll call Nancy is concerned with asking her boss for a raise. Here's how she would go through the Schema Reframe Tool. There are five steps to it:

Step 1. What's going on?

Nancy: "I'm having a hard time speaking with my boss and asking for a raise. Every time I try, I get tongue-tied and give up. I'm starting to feel resentful that I work so hard for so little. I'm beginning to hate going to work."

(We start by just trying to say or jot down the disturbing situation, what is causing the stress).

Step 2. Feel your four core feelings.

Nancy feels:

1. *I feel angry*…"that it's so *&%# hard to speak up! I HATE that I get so scared! I CAN'T STAND that everyone else got that *&^ promotion but me! I am SO PISSED this is so hard for me!"

(Express your anger as fully as you can, until you feel that tender, softer opening in your heart and the natural sadness underneath the anger begins to appear).

2. *I feel sad*…"that I don't feel valued at work. I feel sad that I'm not valuing myself."

3. *I feel afraid*…"that if I speak up I'll be rejected, turned down. I feel afraid that I'll never be able to speak up."

4. *I feel guilty*…"that I'm not supporting myself or trusting myself."

(It's easiest to stick with the four most basic negative feelings: angry, sad, afraid and guilty, and to express them, even if only to yourself).

Step 3. Find your unreasonable expectation.

My unreasonable expectation is: (Pause, and see what arises. It may take a while to see it).

Nancy: "My unreasonable expectation is that I don't really deserve a raise. Other people might, but I don't."

Step 4. Turn it around to become a reasonable expectation and repeat.

Nancy: "I deserve a raise as much as anyone. I DO deserve a raise. I've been working hard. I'm a valuable employee. I can speak up and ask for a raise!"

(It may evolve to a simpler, shorter statement)…"I can speak up for a raise! It's safe for me to speak up and support myself!"

Step 5. Look for the deeper pattern, or schema, that might be getting triggered.

Nancy: "I notice I'm feeling that powerless and helpless feeling again. What schema is being triggered? I can't get my needs met. I'm not good enough!"

My affirmation (mantra or core statement of healing and strength): "I can get my needs met. I CAN get my needs met!"

Find words that resonate, statements that create power and energy in your body. Repeat this powerful phrase (again, making sure it's not just "words," but that you can feel their power in your body) as many times as you can.

Keep repeating the meaningful phrase throughout the day. For instance:

- Before you get out of bed in the morning
- Before you fall asleep at night
- When you are exercising
- When you have some quiet time, driving, meditating, cleaning, etc.
- See if you can feel the truth of what you are saying, imagine it so

- Trust that with repetition and persistence your brain will begin to rewire.

Schema Awareness

Re-wiring schemas is an ongoing process, not a one-shot deal. To make a real impact on those old wires, you need to become more self aware of what gets triggered for you. Most of us have ample material to choose from! The most obvious signs are when you are unusually upset, preoccupied by persistent emotions, having repetitive negative thoughts or feelings or behaving impulsively, aggressively or passively. That's the time to use the Schema Reframe Tool. It's here waiting for you!

Cultivating Curiosity

Curiosity and compassion are two key elements to help your brain move from stress and disconnection back to connection and balance. The next section will offer three strategies for cultivating a curious and compassionate mind. These practices will not only help you when you are triggered, but will help you grow in self-compassion, self-awareness, natural wisdom and resilience.

Curiosity Strategy 1: COAL: Curious, Open, Accepting and Loving

Cultivating a balanced mindset is a powerful tool to support you as you head into a difficult conversation. This mindset, called COAL for short, is worth practicing throughout the day to make it easier to draw upon during difficult conversations. Dan Siegel, in his book *The Mindful Brain*, developed the acronym COAL as a way to describe being mindful, or focusing your awareness on the present moment, moment by moment, to help regulate your emotions and maintain balance.

If this list resonates for you, use it as a daily practice and/or call on it to help you stay in balance during a difficult conversation.

Here are the four qualities of COAL. See if these are qualities you want to cultivate in yourself and if so, how will you remember to do that?

Curious. When you're curious, it means that you have an honest, open-minded desire for discovery and for understanding. You say, "Hmm...I wonder what I will discover as I turn my attention within. Am I getting triggered? What is my stress state? How am I feeling? What do I need?"

Or, you might turn your attention to the other person. "Hmm...I wonder how this other person is feeling or what their stress state is? I wonder what they need?" When you are curious, your fear circuits are deactivated and you can tune in to the present moment with awareness.

Open. Being open means that you have not already decided what the outcome is. It means that you are not certain you are right and they are wrong. When you are open-minded, you are also more likely to be curious and aware. You can be available to new information and can be sensitive to yourself and the other person.

A closed, decided tunnel vision or "certain" mind fuels your default circuits and stress. When you are open, you can allow yourself to notice your feelings and needs, and you can allow yourself to connect with the feelings and needs of the other person.

Accepting. When you are both curious and open, it is easier to be accepting too. Accepting means that you can relax into the moment and accept all of your feelings and the other person's feelings too. You accept and allow this moment, this conversation, to be just as it is.

When you accept the present moment and what's arising, both for yourself and for the other person, it is much easier to stay balanced. You are gathering up information. You are open to new learning and discovery. You are attuned to your own experience, your feelings and needs, as well as the other person's feelings and needs and allowing everything to be as it is. You can more easily let go of judging, trying to fix and change, and trying to control things, all of which fuel stress.

Loving. This final element of COAL is sometimes the hardest. But if you are curious, open and accepting, it's easier to be loving, both toward yourself and all of your feelings and needs, and also to the other person, no matter how different he or she may be. So you can enter into the conversation with respect, and continue to maintain a loving, caring, or respectful approach, even if the feelings get difficult.

If the word "loving" seems too remote, difficult or grandiose, think in terms of "kind awareness," meaning softening the judgment and harshness that all of us can fall into. Imagine the other person as your child, your parent, or your friend, and put the judgments through that conceptual sieve to filter out the harshness. With this kind awareness we shift away from judging, criticizing, condemning, blaming and shaming yourself or another person, and shift towards staying connected whether you are in conflict or not.

These four qualities are about cultivating connection. Connection becomes the deepest foundation that carries you through the most difficult conversations. You are connected first and foremost to yourself. This connection with yourself allows you to connect with others. It is through connection with ourselves that we are able to feel with the other person. As you make this shift, you automatically inoculate yourself against the stress response and against deepening any divisions in heated conversations or moments of conflict.

Curiosity Strategy 2: Put on Giraffe Ears

"Giraffe Ears" is a strategy created by Marshall Rosenberg, the author of *Non-Violent Communication*. This strategy can also help you cultivate a curious and kind mindset when triggered.

To understand what Giraffe Ears are and how to use them, we'll start with two key concepts from Rosenberg: that of Jackal Language and Giraffe Language.

Jackal Language

Jackal is the language of our ego, the inner critic, judge or "gremlin." Our inner Jackal is another name for that part of us that is primitive and gets triggered when we're in stress or conflict. The vagal brake is off and our survival circuitry is on. When your Jackal is in operation you are usually at a lower brain state; it's a sign you have a stressed out brain. Jackal language is the stream of verbiage that you are thinking when you are in that state. It's the blaming, accusing, assuming, attacking kind of thoughts that get activated when you're stressed out. It's certainly not your best self, and Jackal language is most certainly not accurate. It's the mental junk that comes out of a stressed state. The stuff we regret saying and didn't really mean in the first place.

Giraffe Language

Giraffe is the language of compassion. Giraffe Language is the language of feelings and needs. There is no Jackal in a giraffe's vocabulary. We speak Giraffe when our vagal brake is on, when our social engagement system is lit up, and when we are in homeostasis or balance.

Giraffe Ears

Rosenberg was asked once how he survived being in the firing lines of disputes as diverse as race riots in inner-city Detroit and the Middle East conflict. He said:

> *"I never hear what a Jackal-speaking person thinks,*
> *especially what they think about me."*

The challenge in so many difficult conversations is listening to the other person when they are blaming us. We might be blaming them as well. We only have control over ourselves, so let's look at what we have control over.

When you hear someone blaming you, telling you that you've ruined their day, or that it's your fault and you're to blame for their upset, it's hard to maintain a balanced state. It's hard not to take it personally.

However, if you can change the way you are listening, if you can put on your Giraffe Ears and listen like a giraffe does, then you automatically take out the sting and the poison of the harsh words you are hearing.

There are four ways you can think about the blaming messages you are hearing. The first two ways are Jackal-oriented mindsets. The last two are the more life-enhancing and stress-busting Giraffe mindsets.

Choice 1: Hearing Jackal outside—Judging others

When you hear only the angry words someone says to you—their judgments and blaming language—it's natural to blame them back to defend yourself. This way of listening can trigger you further, so hearing Jackal quickly turns to speaking Jackal right back.

When all you hear is Jackal, you need to build a wall of judgment, criticism and blame to defend yourself. Hearing Jackal keeps you stuck in defense mode. Defense mode will disconnect you from the other and cause you to distance.

Choice 2: Hearing Jackal inside–Judging ourselves

This is when you put on "Jackal Ears" and judge yourself. Someone says "You ruined my day"—and you think

83

"You're right. I ruined your day! It's all my fault." That nasty self-critical voice gets activated. The voice of shame. The voice that says "I am bad" or "I am wrong or I'm the problem."

Rosenberg says women tend to be conditioned to blame themselves (Jackal Ears turned inward) and men tend to be culturally trained to have their Jackal Ears turned outward (blaming others).

If you tend to put your Jackal Ears turned inward in conflict and stress, chances are you learned to merge with others in stressful conversations (as opposed to distancing). You feel threatened, and tend to abandon yourself to create a feeling of safety by seeking to please or get approval from others.

Choice 3: Hearing Giraffe outside—Your feelings & needs

You are putting on your Giraffe Ears facing outward when you listen to what the other person's feelings and needs might be. What is important to this person? How are they feeling? What might they need?

As you learn to tune your Giraffe Ears toward the other, you become a compassionate and understanding listener. This act of open-hearted acceptance for the deeper message underneath the blaming, Jackal Language, also creates the safety for the other person to release their own survival-based reactions, and ideally move to a more balanced position in their own brain and communication. The potential for resolution and relationship growth and repair opens up, simply because you are tuning in with your compassionate ears.

Choice 4: Hearing Giraffe inside—My feelings & needs

You can put your Giraffe Ears on facing inward, too. This way, you can give empathy to yourself and hear the message in terms of what is alive in me: What feelings and needs are touched in me when I hear this message? Even knowing that you are getting triggered and being able to identify your reactions requires Giraffe Ears facing inward.

It's interesting to note that most researchers and theorists agree that this inward observation (mindfulness) with compassion for yourself is the launching pad for not only staying connected to yourself in tough conversations, but for you to have true compassion for others and work toward mutually beneficial solutions.

Giraffe Ears inward are in essence the cornerstone of all the tools and techniques for creating "secure attachment" with yourself, and moving forward in your relationships and important endeavors in life.

If your Jackal Ears are activated, you are in an out-of-balance state, and chances are your schemas and defensive patterns have been triggered. Noticing this without judgment and gently but persistently practicing moving back to your Giraffe Ears approach can help build resilience and safer boundaries.

The key to not taking blaming, angry words personally is to remember that when Jackal Language is dominant, all of us feel stress and feel threatened, with childhood schemas activated. You can use your Giraffe Ears to give yourself compassion through hearing your own feelings and needs, and extend that compassion outward by hearing only the other person's feelings and needs—not their stress state thoughts and Jackal Language.

Curiosity Strategy 3: Question Your Reality—Is That True?

Katie Byron has developed a wonderful series of questions to help create a perspective shift when triggered. We've adapted a version of her basic questions for you. Ask yourself these questions when you are upset over a conversation, ruminating, and thinking negatively about yourself, others, or a situation.

First, identify the troubling thought in your mind. Here are some examples:

_____ They are so wrong

_____ I can't speak up

_____ I hate working with this person

_____ They shouldn't treat me like that

_____ It's not fair

Once you have identified your most troubling thought, take it through these questions:

1. How do you feel when you think this thought? (Just say the thought to yourself a few times, and see how it feels in your body).
2. Is this thought really true? Do you absolutely, 100% know that it is really, really true? (Take time here, let it percolate).
3. If not, what is the opposite(s) of this thought?
4. How do you feel when you think this opposite thought?

Here is an example. Let's say the thought is "They shouldn't treat me like this."

1. How do I feel when I think this thought?

Crummy. Angry. Frustrated. Wanting to wring their necks. Powerless. Like a victim. Out of control.

2. Is it absolutely true? Is it 100% absolutely true?

Yes!! They shouldn't!! Well, I guess not 100%. I mean, maybe that's the way others treated them, or maybe they don't have that much of a choice. Maybe it's all they know. Maybe they're stressed.

3. What are the opposites of that thought?

"They should treat me like that!"

Wow! I guess that makes sense if that's all they know and that's what they do in stress.

"I shouldn't treat me like that!"

Ha! That makes me laugh. Yes, I shouldn't treat myself like that because when they said that hurtful thing, I felt badly about myself. In other words, I think this is touching on my own self criticism. I shouldn't treat myself like that!

"I shouldn't treat them like that!"

Ha! Yes I am getting so mad and defensive and honestly hating them right now! Chances are I shouldn't treat them like that!

4. How do I feel when I think this opposite thought?

Oh I feel much better! I feel lighter. I can forgive them. I feel less triggered. I feel like I have the power now to talk to them about how I felt in that communication without blaming them so much or getting defensive!

Mindfulness-in-the-Moment

Mindfulness Strategy 1: Heart Shift Tool

This tool is for you to use right in the moment. It's intended to create a quick shift whenever you start to notice you are feeling triggered and going into a stressed state. You can use this tool when preparing for a difficult conversation or in the heat of the moment. It does require you to have your mindfulness honed well enough that you can catch yourself early in the situation.

This tool helps you support yourself in staying more connected to yourself, more compassionate toward the other person, and to move back to balance.

This tool is expanded and adapted from the HeartMath Institute.

1. Begin by focusing on your breath. Breathe in and breathe out. See if you can breathe right into your heart area. Then breathe out, directly from your heart. Take a few of these nice, deep, heart-based breaths. Notice if you begin to relax a bit. You can put one hand on your heart and the other on your belly for an extra powerful way to bring yourself into your heart and the present moment. If this is all you remember to do when you are triggered, you will already be more balanced than if you didn't do this at all.

2. If you can take one more step, it is very powerful for your mind-heart coherence to bring to mind something or someone you love or appreciate. It could be a person, pet, object, landscape, activity, or anything at all for which you can feel some true, body-based feelings of gratitude, appreciation or love. This starts to change your brain and heart wave patterns. The idea is to focus on this thing you love and breathe into your heart, breathing in the feelings of love, appreciation, and gratitude. Breathe out from your heart, breathing out and surrounding yourself with these feelings of love and appreciation. Take as many of these breaths as you'd like, focusing on these feelings.

You can do this over and over until you calm down and feel more relaxed.

There once were two people who were trying to get through a heated conversation with not much success. They stopped themselves and decided, both of them, to speak to each other while at the same time, putting their own hands over their own hearts. They were doing step one. They then continued on with the rest of the conversation this way. They automatically stopped the stressed-type conversing and started to listen to each other. They were able to come to a resolution quickly and effectively with this one mind-body technique.

We've also invited students in the classroom to try this. Julia has had the privilege of helping hundreds of students over the years to role play difficult conversations. Early on in her career, she would stop these stressed-out individuals and ask them to simply put their hand on their hearts. Or sometimes one hand on their own heart, one on their belly. This technique would quickly shift the dynamic from tense, intense and stressed to calm, connected and clear. It worked every time—and often when only one of them stopped to do it.

You can also use this technique as part of your preparation. Here's how:

1. Imagine this person and see if you can imagine one small thing you love or appreciate about them. It could be anything: the color of their tie, the way they care for their spouse, the way they arrive

to work early every morning, their voice, the kind words they said to you last month, the kind of parent they are.

2. See if you can breathe in and out of your heart, just as you practiced above, and breathe in this small thing you love or appreciate about this person. Breathe it in, and breathe it out, these feelings of gratitude, love, or appreciation. Continue to focus on these feelings of love or appreciation, and use your breath, in and out, until you feel a shift in your energy, perspective or balance. You did it!

Mindfulness Strategy 2: Loving Kindness Meditation

Say you suddenly find yourself barking at your spouse, getting grumpy with your neighbor, or obsessively worrying about your kid. Who knows what got triggered. Maybe you're just tired and cranky. Maybe they looked at you wrong. Maybe there is some deeper-seated schema or unconscious material you are defending against. But sometimes you just want to do something "quick and dirty" to ease up and return to a more decent, open frame of mind and communication.

When you recognize you are triggered, simply follow these words in your mind, over and over, until your mind relaxes and you can be more present.

> May I be safe.
> May my mind be at peace.
> May my body be healthy.
> May my life be of ease and well-being.
> May_____ (the person who triggered you) be safe.
> May their mind be at peace.
> May their body be healthy.
> May their life be of ease and well-being.

This is an adaptation from a Buddhist practice that is very powerful.

Mindfulness Strategy 3: Ho'oponopono

This is a practice that can help soothe the triggered mind. Like the Loving Kindness meditation, just repeating these words over and over until your mind calms down can make a world of difference.

> I love you.
> I'm sorry.
> Please forgive me.
> Thank you.

You say these words even if you aren't feeling the love. The love is for your own hurt vulnerability within, for the love of life, for the love that may be buried at this moment.

"I'm sorry" is a general statement of owning our piece of every difficulty, every sore point or feeling.

"Please forgive me" is about forgiving ourselves and asking for forgiveness from the Spiritual, whatever your belief in the Spiritual may be.

"Thank you" is the universal acknowledgement that just to be alive right now deserves our gratitude, and that although we may not be aware of it in this moment, we have much to be grateful for.

In closing

Know that each and every time you practice one of the tools from this chapter you are literally re-wiring your brain for more peace, joy and compassion. You are changing your automatic reactions to stress, and in essence, growing yourself up!

In the next chapter we will present tools you can use when you plummet down to the full-blown stress response and are in bottom-up processing mode. These are the most difficult times, and we need support and tools to stay cool, hold on to ourselves and minimize the damage of this maximum stress.

CHAPTER 8

TOOLS TO USE FOR THE FULL-BLOWN STRESS RESPONSE

"According to biolinguistics, 'thoughts' are not ideas in our minds--they are conversations that take place within our bodies."

—*Morton Orman*

In the last chapter we introduced tools you can use when you get triggered in difficult conversations or when you find yourself getting upset and disconnecting from yourself and the other person. But what about the times when you drop down to that difficult out-of-balance state, the full-blown stress response? What do you do when you lose your cool completely and can't get yourself to use any of the kind of tools we have talked about so far in this book?

What's Going On?—Splitting from our Wise Self

When your brain is in the full-blown stress response you will be unable to think outside the box, move to listening, or creatively problem-solve. Your brain will be in bottom-up processing and chances are you will be thinking in primitive, black-and-white, all-or-nothing terms. You will be seeing things from a skewed, negative perspective that feels very true. You may go into overwhelm, forgetting your intentions, goals and message. Your brain may shut down; your brain may ramp up. You may lose your voice or express intense anger. You will be in your fight/flight/freeze/submit response.

Remember, when you fall into full-blown stress your vagal brake is off. Your ability to feel connected and balanced and to see life from a wider, more empathic perspective is completely shut down. It's impossible to feel empathy or compassion. Your social engagement system is shut down.

When your brain plummets into full-blown stress, your thoughts and feelings are usually angry, judgmental, punitive, critical, blaming or condemning, (either of yourself or the other person). This is a version of **fight.**

Alternatively, your thoughts and feelings may become panicky, anxious, desperate to escape or avoid; intended to cut yourself off from the other or to put up walls. This is an attempt toward **flight.**

You may find yourself confused, overwhelmed, paralyzed or blank/numb. This is an example of **freeze.**

You may find yourself back-tracking, denying, excusing, trying to placate, and abandoning yourself. Here we have elements of **submit.**

Tools Are Tough to Use in Full Blown Stress

With bottom-up processing you have limited access to your pre-frontal cortex, where you can soothe yourself, bring yourself back to balance and perspective, and calm yourself enough to keep listening, engaged and on the path to healthy solutions.

So, there will be no fancy tools at times like these. Instead, you can only do brief, limited but supportive techniques to help soothe the brain and bring yourself back to relative balance. Here are some ideas on what to do when you get slammed into lower emotional states.

One key to remember is that we all go out-of-balance and into stress, and our best selves are usually very far away for all of us at these times. We've split from our wise self. So the first step is always noticing that you are in full-blown stress, and trying to muster up a bit of understanding or compassion for yourself.

Sure, it means you aren't perfect. But thank goodness you aren't alone. Even the most wise, educated and skillful communicators hit that completely out-of-balance state now and then.

The Safe Separation Tool

When your primitive brain is engaged, you will feel threatened, and in this threatened state it's easy to do damage to your relationships.

In this state, chances are you won't be able to salvage the conversation and get to a mutually beneficial result. Rather, you may say things you don't really mean, hurt the other person, and thwart your ability to move forward in meaningful directions.

If you notice yourself spinning, not thinking clearly, getting defensive, yelling at the other person, (whether in your mind or with your voice), the wisest move may be to stop and create what we call a "safe separation."

A safe separation means you take a moment to acknowledge that you are getting upset, that the conversation is not going anywhere, and that you need some time to cool down and rethink your position.

This is important to understand. No amount of fancy technique is going to help when you are in this state. You need to interrupt the escalation to calm yourself down. The challenge is noticing we are getting as emotionally escalated as we are, and if someone else isn't coaching us to notice, we need to build this capacity in ourselves. It can be achieved with practice.

In a safe separation, the intention is to create space, to interrupt our negative thoughts and interpretations; even if just for a few minutes.

Safe separation is not running away from a conversation. It's common to stop a conversation abruptly by leaving. That is simply a version of flight unless there is a commitment to come back to the matter when calmer.

Safe separation is about acknowledging that nothing good comes from hurting each other and that you need a cooling off period to be able to keep going constructively. It's important, therefore, to commit to coming back to the conversation. Often, it might be that only a few minutes are required to breathe and do some self-soothing techniques—such as discussed in the last chapter.

Here are two examples of what can be said to use the Safe Separation Tool:

"I need a break. I can't listen and I want to. Can we meet again later today?"

"I want to understand but I'm getting too upset to listen well. I am going to need to end this now, but would like to continue our conversation later. Let's meet tomorrow to discuss this more when both of us have had some time to think about this."

Your exact words will depend on if you are talking to your boss or to your spouse or child, but in essence you are setting a boundary so less damage will be done.

Notice how limited the emotional content is in this communication. That's the way it has to be. You are trying to lower your heart rate and use words that will be as neutral as you can to calm yourself and the other person.

Notice as well that a time is suggested to meet again. Sometimes, you might only need a minute to sit still and breathe deeply. In other circumstances, you both might need to take an hour, a day, a week. If both of you are escalating, both of your survival patterns will be activated. The other person may also want to fight, flee, freeze or submit.

This is a practice which will require one of you to enact. For this reason, we recommend memorizing the example words, or memorize other words that work for you. It is important to memorize, as our brains are so limited in full blown stress that it's hard to come up with the right words at the time.

If you are trying to change a close relationship that has a strongly established interactive pattern, you may need to discuss this practice during a quiet time, when you both are in balanced brain states. Let the person know you will be taking these "time outs" with the Safe Separation Tool the next time the difficult conversation or the stressful pattern shows itself. This lets them know that you are not ignoring them, or trying to take attention. You are simply trying something new.

By giving the person a warning that you will not engage in the negative pattern but will be practicing the Safe Separation Tool, it will set you up for more support as you practice. Be prepared: if the old pattern had you getting into knock-down drag-out fights, the first few times you leave to establish a boundary, your partner may get quite upset. Please just continue to practice the tool. Over time he or she will realize that it's time to change this pattern too, and you'll make great headway in creating change. Also, if you prepare them for your Safe Separation Tool use, they will be more likely to acknowledge it without being triggered.

By using the Safe Separation Tool you are creating a boundary in the relationship and the conversation. That boundary is your pause. It gives you time to calm down, use the tools we presented earlier to reframe any schemas or return to a place of mutual listening and problem solving.

You'll be creating a new norm in the relationship, where you don't allow the hurtful comments and difficulties of trying to communicate in the full-blown stress response. No one communicates well in a stressed state.

Creating this boundary is a way of being responsible to the relationship, honoring yourself and the other person. Make sure you let the person know that you are not abandoning them or neglecting them, you are just wanting to move to a place where you can problem solve rather than get stuck in defensive patterns. It is often most helpful to let the other person know when you would like to return to discuss the issue. However, if the difficult conversation pattern has any indications of provoking harm or abuse of any nature-physical, emotional or verbal, please speak to a professional before you try any of these tools.

Inner Damage Control Tool

Sometimes you don't have the opportunity to state out loud what you need with the Safe Separation Tool. Maybe you're in a meeting. Maybe it's a relationship where you don't have that ability or permission to set limits like that. Maybe you can't find the words or are too upset to calmly state your needs at the time.

In these cases, it's best to use a tool that helps you control yourself in an effort to minimize any damage. The Inner Damage Control Tool can also be used to help prevent you from getting to the point where you need to use the Safe Separation Tool. So, this tool is applicable in all situations where you are starting to move into a full-blown stress response.

This is a self-talk, self-soothing tool that can help train your brain to calm itself during tough times in conversations. This particular tool is adapted from Emotional Brain Training.

To practice this tool, simply say these three phrases to yourself, over and over. These three statements are useful to have memorized as well, because you will need to remember them at your most stressed times.

Write these statements down and practice them whenever you find yourself out-of-balance. For example, when you are in traffic and your brain state is stressed or when you wake up or go to sleep at night and your thoughts are stressful and unsettling. By practicing these statements when you are in general stress, they will be easier to recall during your most stressful conversations.

The first statement is **Do Not Judge**.

Since the brain in stress has moved to primitive, black-and-white, all-or-nothing thinking, we will have automatically gotten judgmental. In this out-of-balance state, we will be judging ourselves, the other person, the situation, the organization or the relationship. So by repeating these words, **Do Not Judge,** you are setting a safe limit in your own brain, reminding yourself that your judging thoughts are just a part of the stress response, they aren't real and they aren't helpful.

Say this phrase over and over again until your mind calms just a bit, or you are less attached to and engaged in your critical, judging thoughts.

For instance, let's say you are in a meeting and you think a team member is criticizing your work and steam-rolling the discussion. Let's say you manage to notice that you have not only been triggered, but that you have moved into the full-blown stress response. You have lost perspective, are fuming, and are highly judgmental. Rather than trying to speak up, because you have a sense you will just fight back, you practice damage control. You say to yourself, "**Do Not Judge**." You say it over and over again until you begin to feel your brain calming a bit.

The second statement is Limit the Harm. As your brain and thoughts quiet, move to the next statement: **Limit the Harm.** Say this phrase a few times too. As you calm down, you can ask yourself what the phrase might mean to you in that moment. Many times limiting harm will mean refusing to believe any negative thoughts. Often it will mean "zip your lip," or don't say the mean or angry statements that are going through my mind. Sometimes minimizing harm means refraining from old habits of hurting yourself or others. As you say these words silently you can begin to put into practice whatever they mean to you in the moment.

The third statement is Know This Will Pass. When we go into full-blown stress we will find ourselves using words like "always" and "never" ("He always picks a fight," "This will never get better"). This is just an expression of the tunnel vision and black-and-white thinking of the brain in stress. The truth is that this stress state will pass. You will be able to communicate again. You will feel better. Remind yourself by saying the phrase **Know This Will Pass.** This phrase reminds you of the falsehood of believing this state will last forever. It will not. It will pass.

Repeat these three phrases to yourself, over and over, until you have quieted your brain enough to get through the moment, minimizing the damage of the brain trying to communicate in stress.

The Witness Tool

When we can maintain even a slight degree of curiosity and compassion it can help circumvent the amygdala's fear response. This is the act of witnessing, where we have one molecule observing our experience with curiosity and compassion. It takes moving your attention in the moment back to your body and breath. You simply notice you are breathing. Maybe you notice your breath has become more shallow or more rapid. *"Oh dear, isn't this interesting, look how I am feeling and what is happening in my body."*

Curiosity will help you later pick up a tool to do a schema reframe or strengthen your skill in self-awareness and self-regulation. You step out of the blaming/shaming game by just noticing. *"Wow, I wonder what's come up for me that I've gotten so triggered."*

You try to connect to your own experience in the moment with some compassion. *"I must be really upset here…it's Ok to get upset sometimes… it's natural…"*

When you are practicing witnessing, you will be better able to coach yourself through a situation. As in the above example: *"I must be really upset here…it's OK to get upset sometimes…it's natural…hmm…what do I need…breathe, breathe a few times, those nice deep breaths…I need to calm myself down, do not judge…limit the harm…"*

When you merge with your experience it is more difficult to find that inner voice of calm and clarity to support you through the moment.

Remember, no one's perfect. We all get triggered. Our growth and learning comes from noticing these triggers and building skills to move forward beyond our early schemas and self-limiting beliefs.

If you practice the act of witnessing, and being open and accepting of all of your feelings and tendencies, it provides a context for growth and change. If you judge yourself, resist what you're noticing or constrict your body and feelings, it only reinforces the stress response.

Take Care of Yourself So You Are Less Vulnerable to Full-Blown Stress

When it comes to handling the stress response, you can highly influence how stressed you get, how easy it is to get triggered, and how "low you go" by how well you take care of yourself and your body.

When you are hungry, tired, or numb from too much screen time in a stiff body, you will be more vulnerable to emotional, relationship, or communication stress. If you have a schedule where you are busy with one task after another, rushing from here to there without breaks or time outs for self care, you will be more vulnerable to going out-of-balance and into the stress response. If you haven't taken time for rest, nature, art and creativity, exercise, play and fun, you will be more vulnerable to stress and it will show up in communication and relationships.

Taking care of yourself and your body creates an inoculation against the stress response. You will be less frequently triggered and will be better able to move back to balance when you are triggered. It is important that you are rested, nourished and that your biological needs are cared for. Not only can good health strengthen your vagal brake, it creates a generally supportive biological platform from which springs all mindfulness and self-control.

The basic biological needs we are talking about are these:

- Plenty of restful, restorative sleep.
- Healthy nutrition—plenty of nutrient dense, organic, plant based foods, grass fed and pasture raised proteins, organic fruits and nuts, fish.
- Adequate fresh water intake.
- Sufficient levels of exercise and movement.
- Creative pursuits, hobbies, passions.
- Time in nature, listening to music, dancing, enjoying the arts.
- Relaxation and spiritual time, meditation, prayer, worship.
- Community time—connecting with others, sharing, laughter, support.

Science suggests that the lifestyle elements listed above are important in keeping you resilient to stress.

If this seems like a hefty list, don't worry. You don't have to do it all at once, or perfectly. Just building in a few practices each week that begin to meet these basic biological needs will help.

When your body is in balance, your neurochemistry is in better balance, and it becomes easier to stay in balance no matter what life throws your way. Difficult conversations are inevitable. By taking care of yourself, by putting your well-being on the front burner, you are better able to navigate through hot conversations and stay relatively cool.

Rework Unreasonable Expectations to Decrease Stress

One thing that can throw all of us into a tail-spin and keep us in lower emotional states are our "unreasonable expectations."

It's easy to walk around in life carrying a load of these expectations consciously and unconsciously; usually we aren't even completely aware of it. These weigh on us like an invisible, but very heavy, backpack. You become more vulnerable to reacting and falling into full-blown stress when you are loaded down with these expectations.

These unreasonable expectations are often linked to your schemas, so as you identify and get clearer on your schemas, your unreasonable expectations will become clearer and vice versa.

Here are a few examples of unreasonable expectations or faulty beliefs we see over and over again in our work:

"I should never get angry. No one should ever get angry with me".

"Conflict is not safe. It's better to avoid conflict at all cost".

"If I get upset, it means I'm a bad person".

"I'm supposed to be perfect. I have to be perfect to be OK".

"If there's a disagreement, someone is right and someone is wrong. I am the right one."

"If there's a conflict, it means something bad will happen. It's not OK, I'm not safe."

"If they disagree with me it means I'm wrong. Or less-than. If I disagree with them, it means they are stupid. Or bad. Or less-than."

You can see that if a challenge comes up in a conversation and you are unconsciously holding on to one of these expectations, it can easily plummet you into stress, where it will be difficult to hang in there, hang on to yourself, and keep communicating in a productive way.

So one key is to notice if you are holding on to any unreasonable expectations about conflict, anger, upset or negative feelings. Or perhaps you are holding unreasonable expectations about yourself and others. Remember every human being goes out-of-balance and into stress at times. It comes out in our communication and relationship patterns. It is normal and OK.

Your job is to notice your tendencies and build your skills to lessen the hurt and pain that can come from these stressed out moments. Your job is to forgive yourself and others and move forward resolving problems and speaking up as best you can.

Cultivate a Kind Inner Voice

Are you aware of the nature and tone of your inner voice? It's surprisingly common for this inner voice to be harsh, critical, anxious, or self-deprecating. We recommend taking a serious look at developing a kinder, more understanding inner voice. It's one of the keys to holding on to yourself through conflict.

But first you have to grow in awareness about the nature and tone of your own inner voice. Here are some questions to ask yourself:

- Do you have a harsh, punitive, judgmental inner voice?
- Is there a voice inside that speaks loud and clear when difficulties come up; one that tends to be unforgiving, shaming, blaming, abusive or abandoning?

- When you get into conflict or a difficult conversation, do you tend to observe yourself from outside of yourself and see your flaws and inadequacies in glaring detail?
- Do you tend to say things like this to yourself? "Now look what you did, you really screwed this one up," "they are laughing at you, they think you are an idiot," or "oh no, they can see what a flake you are, how incompetent."

If you answered yes to any of these questions you are not alone! This tendency to drop into a harsh and critical inner voice tends to begin early in life, and it's a tendency whose intention is good…to keep you safe and to optimize your survival growth. However, this inner voice's methods are flawed.

Just like training a puppy or teaching a child, you must provide a context of support and encouragement rather than punishment and humiliation. We learn best in this environment. Often we can apply this when we are housebreaking our cute golden retriever or helping our niece or neighbor, but it is difficult applying it to ourselves.

This is fundamental in learning to stay cool during heated conversations. Adopting and strengthening a kind inner voice is vital; one that is empathic towards yourself and that knows your strengths and believes in you.

Your inner dialogue can either be a buffer against the full-blown stress response, or it can be a catalyst to send us plummeting out-of-balance. A small conflict comes up, and that voice can fuel it into full-blown crisis, or cool it down to just a mild blip of a disturbance. All of this just by how we speak to ourselves!

Making a firm commitment to noticing when your harsh and punitive voice arises, and gently but persistently turning it around, is crucial to supporting yourself away from full-blown stress. Remember the harsh voice's intention is to help you, so don't judge and criticize yourself for judging and criticizing yourself!

Rather, thank that voice for its intention, and see what your kinder, more nurturing inner voice has to say. The idea is this: you are practicing having empathy for yourself, and being on your own side.

For example, let's say you make a significant mistake at work. Ouch. But as your punishing, blaming inner voice kicks in *("Geez, what an idiot, I can't believe you did that. You're going to get fired")* just notice it, take a breath, and then see if you can feel some compassion for yourself. You don't want to beat yourself up for having that harsh voice, or for the mistake. See if you can simply feel the pain of not being perfect. See if you can remember that none of us are perfect and mistakes happen. See if you can muster a bit of perspective *(it feels crummy now, but this will pass)*. You can practice damage control at this time, too.

Another way to strengthen that kind inner voice is to practice the part of the Centering Tool which suggests you give yourself a kind or supportive message a few times a day. This can be a practice you decide to take on for a period of time: to pause throughout the day and give yourself encouraging, heart-felt messages. That may be the only times in the day when you are truly speaking to yourself in an intentionally kind voice. It's a great start!

Create Your Own Personal Safety Guidelines

Although you can't develop these in the moment of a full-blown stress response, it's important to develop your own set of rules to help you navigate those most stressful times. We suggest you decide upon a set of rules that you spell out for yourself and remind yourself of over and over until they become habits or norms. Like all steps when you are in full blow stress, your phrases need to be short, simple and easy to remember.

Having your own personal conduct rules means *I just don't do that. I don't go there. I don't allow for that to happen.* Then, no matter what, you commit yourself to these rules.

Here are some examples of such rules that some of our clients have made a commitment to. You can experiment and explore to see if any of these fit for you, or if there are others that are important to you.

- I do not hit or physically attack another. I do not tolerate any physical attack from another.
- I do not name-call. I do not accept name-calling from another.
- I do not swear at another person. I will not be sworn at.

- When I completely lose my cool and go into rage, I leave the room or exit as quickly as I am able. I commit to resume in a calmer tone.
- When I feel unsafe or attacked by another, I exit the conversation as quickly as I am able. I commit to resume in a calmer tone.
- I do not solve communication problems by "triangulating" or complaining about one person to another. If I have a problem, I expect myself to speak directly to the person involved.

It's not that you have to be perfect with these rules. However, they will provide some structure and safety for you in relationships and conversations. If you get clear on your rules, articulate them and begin practicing them, you will strengthen your ability to hold on to yourself.

Please take a moment to design your own personal guidelines. As you practice, you'll get better able to implement them and this will help buffer you against the potential ravages of stressful conversations.

Trust the Full-Blown Stress Response

It's easy to jump to negative conclusions about the full-blown stress response. But it's built into our wiring and neurobiology. It's not about good and bad, it's about the perception of worthiness, safety, value, belonging and survival. It's about each of us and our journey toward wholeness, creative self-expression and making a difference in the world.

Each stress state, even the full-blown one when our feelings and thoughts are the most ramped up and negative, has its purpose as well as its rewards and challenges. Without the full-blown stress response, we would not have survived as a species.

So if you can adopt a more kind and welcoming position you will be moving forward in your own development and growth. Live with empathy and an open heart while you continue to set loving limits on how you act and how you communicate during these times of survival instinct. Trust your inherent goodness and worthiness, know you don't have to be perfect or even better than you are to be lovable, worthy and of value. By trusting your body and your deepest self, you can strengthen your skills and refine your approach to all kinds of difficult conversations.

CHAPTER 9

REPAIR IS HEALING AND STRENGTHENING

"The quality of our lives depends not on whether or not we have conflicts, but on how we respond to them."
—*Tom Crum*

We all are going to get triggered into stress in conversations, and the more engaged, active and vibrant our lives, the more potential chances we have to get triggered.

We also will fall into the full-blown stress response at times, when we are tired or hungry or already slightly stressed, when the stakes are high and our schemas make us vulnerable, or when we are caught off guard. This is a fact of life, a part of the human condition, and it is a reasonable expectation.

So in addition to having a tool belt to use during tough conversations, one of the important things to learn and practice is how to *repair* relationship hurts—and how to strengthen and heal important connections following stressful, triggering events.

This chapter will present tools and techniques you can practice to help you repair important relationships after difficult, wounding conversations.

After a Melt Down

When a melt down happens and you've fallen into full-blown stress, chances are elements of the conversation broke down and hurt both you and the other person. Angry or upset feelings were triggered and damage has been done. Hopefully, you had a chance to use a tool such as the Schema Reframe or the Safe Separation Tool. Hopefully you got some space to help yourself move out of the stress response before tackling the issue or approaching the person again.

Remember, it's not YOU, it's not THEM. It's the brain in stress.

Studies suggest that it is not the stressful conversation itself that matters most. You will go into low brain states in all relationships and difficult, stressed-out conversations can and do happen. What's most important, especially in your long-term, interdependent relationships, is the repair work following the upset. The repair work strengthens the relationship ties and supports restoring the relationship in the future.

So after a melt-down, if it's reasonable to expect that repair can happen (and that it will be good for the relationship and the situation) it is wise and powerful to approach the other with the intention of healing and repair.

A criteria to check before you do so is to ask yourself, am I in balance? Or, have I used my tools to get back to balance so I can truly listen, and stay attuned to my own feelings and needs? Approaching the other person while you are still in the grips of stress will usually only add fuel to the fire. Bring yourself to a more balanced state first.

Ask Yourself About Risks and Benefits

Once you feel more calm, here are some questions to consider in deciding whether you want to go forward and make a repair plan:

1) Is it important to you to repair?
2) Does this relationship matter and does the subject area matter?
3) Given this person, given the situation, is it reasonable to expect that something good can come out of repair?

If the answers to these questions are YES, then it is most likely worth it to gather up your inner resources and approach the person.

Here's one more question to ask:

4) What are the risks of having this repair conversation? What are the benefits? We tend to put a lot of effort into thinking about all the risks in bringing up a topic, but not much thought into what the benefits might be. Make time to list those benefits to offset the risks, which are often greater in our minds than in reality. What are the realistic benefits of risking this conversation?

How Do You Repair?

We recommend the following to create a repair plan:

Press the Reset Button

Step 1. Prepare Yourself: Prepare yourself by connecting with your best intentions and your own heart. That is, reconnect with what you value about the person and the relationship, and how you want to feel and behave in connection with him or her. Here are some questions to help you do that:

- Can I see this person clearly, acknowledging their value and perspective? Can I feel respect for them and their inherent worthiness? Do I need to work on letting go of judgment, blame, shame, fear, the need to control or any other blocks to connection? Have I acknowledged and released (to the best of my abilities) any schemas that were triggered for me? Am I aware of the other person's needs?
- Can I see my own value and worthiness? Can I hold myself with self-respect and value in this situation without taking on the other person's perceived blaming of me? Have I clarified my deepest need for myself in this situation?

- Have I connected with how I want to feel about this person, myself and the situation? Can I see the possibility of mutual needs, gains or benefits? Or, if I can't see any possibility yet, am I willing to hang in there with the person until we can find common ground?
- Have I imagined the conversation going well? Do I believe it will go smoothly and make it through tough moments to achieve the outcome I'm looking for?

Step 2. Set the Stage. Once you have your mind and heart aligned, approach the other person to ask for a time that is mutually acceptable. Let the other person know what the topic is that you'd like to discuss more deeply.

Step 3. Open with Appreciation. Once you've agreed upon a time to meet to discuss the topic that began the conflict, it's important to set an appreciative and collaborative tone right at the start. Research done by John and Julie Gottman shows that the first few minutes of a conversation predict how it will turn out. So intentionally start with something you authentically appreciate about the other person or your relationship. For example: "Thank you for meeting with me again to finish our work on the project."

Step 4. Be Vulnerable—Share Your Feelings and Needs. This would sound something like:

> *"I feel sad that we had such a difficult time last week when we tried to create a timeline. I need you to know that your perspective is important to me."* Or, *"I'm worried that we never really got resolution in our conversation yesterday. I need to see if you'd be willing to try again."*

Step 5. Express Your Desire to Start Again—For instance: *"I'd like to start again and see if we can find a mutually beneficial solution."*

Get Curious About Their Feelings and Needs

It can help to become curious about what the other person might be feeling or needing. You can work on this in your own mind, and use your intuition to sense the person's feelings and needs, or you can ask the person directly. It could sound something like:

> *"I know we had a difficult conversation yesterday. Working with you toward positive outcomes is very important to me. I'd like to better understand how you are (or were) feeling about the project, and what you need. Would you mind taking a few minutes to share with me these two things, how you feel and what you need? Again, it's important for me to understand where you're coming from."*

The Apology

Apologies are sometimes due if there has been a mistake or genuine harm done, damaging trust. Apologies can be over-rated and sometimes people can fear that apologizing makes them culpable.

With all the fear of blaming and shaming attached to apologizing, it is no wonder that it is hard to do. However, an apology can also be a very powerful and moving way to repair and restore relationships.

Apologies are both art and science. Usually, we recommend keeping it simple. It helps to use Giraffe Ears, own your part of the problem and present your intention for a better outcome this time. Then, begin listening openly again.

> *"I'm sorry for the way that conversation went yesterday and my part in it. I'm wondering if we can begin again. This time I'd like to do a better part in listening and understanding your perspective."*

The Honoring Differences Tool

Sometimes no resolution is in sight and the issue needs to rest until things change enough for the topic area and situation to evolve. In cases like this, you can agree to disagree, or choose to let go of needing a certain outcome for the time being. With repair, it will still be important to address the conflict directly.

> *"I regret the way that conversation went yesterday. I think we both are passionate about this situation, and we obviously see things differently. I would like to suggest that we just sit with this for a while, and see how things unfold. Our working relationship is important to me, and I wouldn't want this conflict to chip away at that."*

Keep Doing Your Inner Work

The more you can become aware of your schemas, and of what sends you into full-blown stress, the more able you'll be to circumvent melt downs or prevent difficult conversations from turning into nightmares. Most of us have tendencies that fall into themes or patterns. So the Schema Reframe Tool may come back into necessity time and again. We are all works in progress. Learning about what sends you into stress is an ongoing process.

Are there conditions that set you up for dropping into stress? Not enough sleep? Too much on your plate? Skipped lunch and stomach is growling? When you've been over focused on the computer or a project for hours and are grouchy, tired, body aching? All of these biological set-ups can throw you into the stress response.

Self-awareness, self-compassion, compassion towards others, trust, commitment to authenticity and honesty, the ability to forgive or at least move on, and a general positive expectancy toward relationships and conflict can all help create the basis for healthy connections and conversations—and for holding on to yourself when things get challenging.

What To Do When You're Not Sorry and You Can't Let It Go

Sometimes the conversation hurt so badly, or was so difficult, that it feels virtually impossible to forgive and let go.

If you are facing such a situation, relax. It's normal. You may need to feel hurt and angry for a long time before the situation rights itself, or it becomes water under the bridge. If you've tried using tools to rewire schemas, if you've seen what your deeper needs are that aren't being met, if you are bringing self -awareness into the situation but it's not resolving inside your own inner life, then it may be time to breathe, relax, and practice some self-acceptance. You may need to simply say to yourself: *"I will let myself be as angry as I need to be for as along as I need to."*

You can't make your feelings go away, but you can set limits on your behavior. If this is a work or family relationship that requires some basic civility and on-going interactions, then it's important to set limits on your communication and behavior.

For instance, you may need to remind yourself to avoid the topic that creates the conflict, or agree to leave the room if the person tries to re-engage in the conflict. You may need to practice polite, superficial communication for the time being, the bare minimum of what your job or relationship requires. You may need to remind yourself to still listen to the person, give eye contact, nod and be civil, and to be professional, even if you don't feel like it at all.

In time, as your feelings calm (time continues to be a wonderful healer!) you can consider going back to repair any relationship damage. Then you can take on the conflict and communication again, or decide to let it go once and for all.

It helps to have a journal to express your anger and frustration, or to confide in a trusted friend. It usually does not help to triangulate, or vent to other people involved in the situation or connected to the issue. Triangles create more problems, so if you need to have some time to vent and clarify your feelings, find someone who is not connected to the situation. Don't use someone in your family if it's a family issue, or don't use someone who works for your organization if it's in your work community.

Being Sensitive to Other's Stress

It's important to remember that we all have the tendency to fall into stress states, and to suffer from the effects of stress on our thoughts, feelings and behavior. It can be helpful to practice noticing where your colleagues and family members are on the stress scale. If they are in lower brain states, triggered, or in full-blown stress, then you want to notice this and adapt your expectations.

When others are out-of-balance and in full-blown stress, please remember:

1. **They aren't thinking clearly.** Don't take their words to heart. They will be thinking in negative, black-and-white, emotional, or all-or-nothing terms. Remember, they don't necessarily believe what they are saying in that moment. It can help to remember that they didn't really mean that painful thing they just said to you. They were speaking from their lower stress state and it's not all of who they are. It's not even a dominant part of who they are. They are much, much more than that. Marshall Rosenberg used to say that he never listened to the "Jackal" spewing of damaging thoughts that came from people's mouths in those upset states. He only listened to people's feeling and needs. That's the essence of Giraffe Ears.

2. **They have ramped up feelings.** Don't try to talk them out of their feelings, they don't have a choice right now, and won't be able to process your good advice. Don't tell them they shouldn't be feeling what they are feeling. Don't share with them ideas on how to fix things when they are upset. And don't point out the silver linings in their situation. As Brene Brown says, it's not time to say "At least you have…" It's not time to show them the brighter side of life. All you can do is listen respectfully, and try not to get triggered to a lower state yourself. You may need to set a boundary, a Safe Separation, and ask to discuss this at a later time if the conversation feels unproductive and you are worried you might get triggered if you don't end it soon.

3. **Their listening skills are turned off.** Due to the stress response, their brain has taken on tunnel vision, and they will not be able to listen to and process much of what others are saying. It's not their fault. It's literally a function of stress hormones. Adapt your expectations and don't waste your breath.

4. **Chances are they will cool down and be able to discuss this again.** It's OK to come back to the topic later once everyone has cooled down. Others who are ramped up and at a lower state might not like you setting a limit (we get a dopamine charge when we can get others engaged in the battle) but it will help with damage control and to minimize the damage of lower state communication.

Watch out for getting your stress response triggered when the other person is stressed out. When others come at you angry, upset, afraid, or however their own schemas and stress is showing up, you will be vulnerable to having your own stress states activated.

Create a safe boundary. Just because they are in the stress response doesn't mean you have to automatically go there with them. Use your breath, your positive self statements, your tools in connecting to yourself and your Giraffe Ears to try to stay present, listening and supportive. Do not buckle and fall into the mire of stress, too.

The Key to Growth Lies in Repairing and Restoring

As you know, we all get triggered and we all get stressed. We all have a particular thumbprint, as well as general similarities when we go into a full-blown stress response. It's the social mammalian brain. It's our neurobiology. It's our wiring.

They key to our growth and to the healthy development of our relationships, both intimate and professional, is our ability to move through stress and return to homeostasis—to re-enter into dialogue and to repair and restore and move forward.

Holding on to yourself means strengthening that ability to come back and clean up past upsets. It means trusting yourself and the other person enough, valuing yourself and the other person enough, to do the difficult job of repair.

We say difficult, because sometimes it feels risky to return to a conversation and admit one's mistakes. It is not easy to take responsibility for one's own stress response, or to own up to not being perfect or right all the time. It takes courage to forgive, to admit weaknesses and mistakes, to open your heart and mind and listen again.

But this is what our emotional and spiritual growth is all about, as well as the healthy development of our families, communities and organizations. This is what the evolution of our species and effective problem-solving require.

So each time you take the time to move back to that state of balance, clarity, compassion and understanding, each time you return to repair and restore, to clear up a difficult communication, you are nourishing yourself, others and your organization.

As Gandhi said, you are being the change you want to see in the world.

CHAPTER 10

TOOLS TO USE WHEN YOU ARE IN BALANCE

"All that we are is the result of what we have thought. It is founded on our thoughts...if one speaks or acts with a pure thought, happiness follows one, like a shadow that never leaves."

—The Buddha

As we were finishing up this book, several colleagues and clients asked the following: "What tools can we use when we are in balance, and want to deepen our skills and keep ourselves there?"

That's a great question, as sustaining and deepening your higher brain state experience gives your brain the message that it's safe to be open, it's safe to be loving and it's safe to be yourself, just as you are. As you know, the more time you spend triggered or in full-blown stress, the more easily your brain will go there and potentially get stuck in a lower set point.

The good news is, it works the opposite way too. The more you can allow and enjoy the good feelings and connections emanating from a balanced state, the more you will find yourself experiencing that state, and the more you are priming your brain to go there.

So here are some tools and practices you can use to strengthen and expand the times of balance in your life. The time to practice these tools is when you are in a state of balance.

Recognize the State: Mindful Awareness

As usual, the starting point is to be mindful and aware of your state. Recognize when you are actually in a balanced state. There are many moments throughout each and every day when we are all in those states. Notice those times, put your attention on your body, feel your breath, feel the good feelings in your body.

What are those good feelings? In a nutshell, look for feelings that are grateful, happy, secure, peaceful, loved and loving, healthy, relaxed, connected, supported, content, and whole.

Identify the feelings that are present in your state of balance. Feel the body sensations accompanying those feelings. Breathe.

Laurel Mellin, in *Wired for Joy*, calls these moments "joy points." Rick Hanson calls it "soaking in the good."

These moments seal in the neurochemistry of well-being.

Breathing Compassion Tool

When you find yourself enjoying a balanced, good-feeling state, a terrific way to deepen and strengthen the wires of joy and contentment is to practice this tool. Simply breathe in and feel compassion. Breathe out and send that compassion out to others.

Breathe in and feel the compassion in your body. Send that compassion to every cell of your body. Relax.

Breathe out and send that compassion out to someone special in your life who needs it. Or send that compassion out to a group of people, your neighbors, friends, family or work team. Best of all, breathe out and send that compassion out to all living things. Relax.

Deepen the Feelings of Gratitude and Appreciation

When we're in a higher brain state it is far easier to really feel our good feelings. We don't have to fake it, or try to find them, or think about what might be good in our life. We can experience the body sensation, the presence of well-being and joy.

Two of the most powerful positive feelings that rewire our brain are gratitude and appreciation. So simply take a moment, when you realize you are in balance and feeling good, to become aware of your breath, your body and feelings. Bring up that feeling of gratitude. Let yourself finish this statement, as many times as you want:

I feel grateful for...

See if you can feel the grateful feeling for whatever is present and true in your life. Be grateful for whatever your mind lands on, or even if your mind doesn't land on anything, just feel the feeling of gratitude. Breathe.

I appreciate...

What are you appreciating about your life right now? It might be simple, like the warm socks on your feet, the birds chirping outside, the sound of the breathing of a loved one besides you. See if you can bask in the feeling.

Check in With Your Feelings and Needs Tool

When in homeostasis we usually don't experience ourselves as having any profound needs. Maybe simple things like "I feel thirsty, I need water" or "I have a full bladder, I need a restroom" come up, but in general we are humming along, connected to ourselves and aligned with our purpose and well being.

Small little dips in homeostasis are important to attend to, as it protects us from plummeting into the triggered or full-blown stress states.

So checking in with your feelings and needs can be very useful for helping yourself stay at a higher, in-balance state.

How do I feel? Maybe you are busy at your computer and you begin to feel a little achy or tired. What do I need? I need to stretch, get up and move around a bit, get some water.

Or let's say you are eating dinner with a friend, and you notice that you are starting to get antsy. Ask yourself, how do I feel? I feel annoyed, irritated. What do I need? I need to let go of my judgment and just listen. Or I need to speak up and correct that misunderstanding.

Or perhaps you are thinking of your next day or another future event. What are you feeling as you think about it? What does that tell you about what you might need?

By asking yourself throughout the day these basic questions—How do I feel? What do I need?—you are doing little bits of inner housekeeping. Clearing up clutter. Getting rid of potential trash and toxins. Keeping a clear and connected inner life. All of these things help you to stay in balance and at that ease-full state of balance and joy.

Balanced Lifestyle Tools

One of the best ways to help yourself experience more balanced states and maintain and sustain those states is to take care of your basic lifestyle needs.

We are wired for tribal closeness, and in the modern world we have the danger of too much isolation. Be sure to get your needs for emotional connection, loving touch, laughter and shared activities met.

We are wired for periodic physical stress, and these days we have chronic emotional stress, so be sure to get plenty of physical movement and activity to balance these disparate types of stress.

We are wired for healthy, nature-made foods and unfortunately we have an abundance of unhealthy, man-made food too easily available. Be sure to limit the junk and get plenty of healthy nutrients.

We are wired for relaxation, restoration and down time. Nap, lounge, day dream. Whatever your favorite ways are to unwind and relax, practice them daily!

Finally, don't forget all of those components of stress-buffering lifestyle tools we mentioned earlier: nature, pets, art, music, creativity, gardens, meditation, play, working with your hands, singing, dancing, inspired reading, prayer, and soulful passions.

All those things that bring your brain to ease, balance and joy. Practice them!

CHAPTER 11

HOLDING ON TO YOURSELF

"Every conflict we face in life is rich with positive and negative potential. It can be a source of inspiration, enlightenment, learning, transformation, and growth—or rage, fear, shame, entrapment, and resistance. The choice is not up to our opponents, but to us, and our willingness to face and work through them."
—Kenneth Cloke and Joan Goldsmith

We hope this book has given you some insight and tools to help you stay cool and hold on to yourself when conversations get hot. Holding on to yourself means staying connected within—staying attuned to your own feelings and needs, to your intention and your sense of value and worthiness, and to your ability to be open and caring. Holding on to yourself means staying connected to your heart, to have empathy and understanding of others and to see and work toward positive outcomes.

As you've learned, this requires being in balance and having a brain that is relaxed and present. It requires lowering your own stress response and stress hormones. It means having your vagal brake on.

The good news is, the more you practice moving out of a stress state to a more balanced state the more you are priming your brain to naturally move towards balance. You are changing your emotional or stress set point. The more you practice the tools we have presented here, the more your brain will be resilient to stressors and conflict.

It Takes Practice

It takes commitment and practice. We all fall into the stress response, and the more important the relationship and topic, the more vulnerable we are to going out-of-balance when conversations get heated. But as you build these skills you will be able to move more quickly back to balance. You'll be able to discern when others are in lower states and adjust your expectations. You will be able to go back and repair relationships whenever it is in the best interest of all concerned.

Doing the Ground Work

The more you can strengthen your self-awareness and practice self-compassion, the easier it will be to hold on to yourself. This requires knowing who you are and what you truly value in life. It means releasing "shoulds," or the tendency to seek approval, safety and worthiness outside of yourself. It means deepening your relationship with the spiritual—however you experience and define that. It means moving forward from a place of trust and safety, and relying on that deepest connection with yourself and life.

There's a reason why so many spiritual traditions recommend meditative practices, as they shift our focus away from the busy mind and onto our breath and our body, where that feeling of safety and well-being reside. If we identify with our thoughts and emotions too much we will get stuck on the wheel of stress and conflict. When we realize that there is a deeper awareness beneath our transitory thoughts and emotions, then we can connect with our true nature.

There's a reason why spiritual traditions promote techniques to help us connect back with our hearts. The wisdom of the heart, that touchstone of the vagal brake, will be most able to lead us through difficulties in communication.

Each Voice Matters

Each individual voice adds to the creative problem solving and evolution of our teams, organizations and families. We all have value and worthiness. It is important for each person to have the support and skills they need to speak up and add to the dialogue.

We are hoping that this book will help give you the tools and support you need to hold on to yourself and stay in balance in your difficult conversations.

Our greatest growth and potential comes from that which triggers us, that which is difficult. We dedicate this book to your growth, your potential, and the valuable addition you make to all of your relationships and connections.

Our vision is to help you hold on to yourself, strengthen your resilience to stress so you can move through conflict and challenging conversations in positive ways and to help you build healthy and strong families and organizations.

Your voice matters!

Julia Menard has helped thousands of individuals and teams engage in conflict productively. She is a skilled mediator, coach, and trainer who specializes in conflict resolution and difficult conversations. Julia's been practicing for over twenty years and is a key thought leader in her field.

Julia is a mother, dog lover, and lives in the beautiful province of British Columbia.

Judy Zehr is an award-winning writer and mental health expert with over thirty years experience helping individuals, couples, and families learn tools to create more balance and joy in their lives.

Judy has four grown kids and loves to be in the natural environment of her beautiful state of Oregon.

TOOLS

Here is a list of the tools we have mentioned in the book. We hope this list will provide you with a handy way to access and put the tools into practice.

Chapter 2: To Simplify: Three States
   Tool 1) What's Your Stress Set Point?

Chapter 3: We Disconnect in Stress
   Tool 2) Five Practices to Strengthen the Vagal Brake
   Tool 3) Awareness Tool: Do I Distance, Merge or Both?
   Tool 4) Boundary Tool for Self-Differentiation

Chapter 4: Mindfulness Practices
   Tool 5) A Taste of Mindfulness Practice
   Tool 6) Wheel of Awareness Practice
   Tool 7) Centering Tool
   Tool 8) Sense Based Mindfulness Tool
   Tool 9) Emotions Based Mindfulness Tool
   Tool 10) Labeling Needs Mindfulness Tool

Chapter 5: Use Mindfulness to Identify Your Stress States
   Tool 11) What is Your Unique Stress Thumbprint?

BRAIN STATES AND STRATEGIES— CHEAT SHEET

Stress State and Brief Description	Tools to Use for This Stress State
In Balance Balanced; positive feelings, Adaptive, healthy thoughts and behaviors. Feel connected, whole, content	Breathing Compassion Tool Gratitude and Appreciation Check In With Your Feelings and Needs Tool Balanced Lifestyle Tools
Triggered Triggered: negative feelings arising, thoughts get a bit more negative or more extreme, actions teetering on habitual, numbing, anxious, unhealthy. Feel concerned, confused, annoyed, irritated, worried etc.	Schema Reframe Tool COAL Giraffe Ears Question Your Reality HeartShift Tool Loving Kindness Meditation Ho'oponopono

Out-of-Balance Out-of-Balance: ramped up negative feelings and thoughts, black-and-white, all-or-nothing extreme thinking, unconscious patterns and schemas arise, negative unhealthy behaviors connected to fight/flight/freeze/submit reactions	Safe Separation Tool Inner Damage Control Tool The Witness Tool Rework Unreasonable Expectations Kind Inner Voice Safety Guidelines
Creating A Context for Change Tools you can use as a general practice that help "rewire your brain" for less reactivity and resilience to stress	Practices to Strengthen the Vagal Brake Wheel of Awareness Practice All Mindfulness Practices Centering Tool All Schema Awareness Tools Balanced Lifestyle Tools

REFERENCES AND RESOURCES

Chapter 1
Blake, Robert. & Mouton, Jane. *The Managerial Grid Model: The Key to Leadership Excellence*. Houston: Gulf Publishing Co, 1964.

Kraybill, Ray. Style Matters: http://www.riverhouseepress.com/index. php?option=com_content&view=article&id=70&Itemid=512

Thomas-Kilmann Conflict Styles: http://www.kilmanndiagnostics.com/ overview-thomas-kilmann-conflict-mode-instrument-tki

Chapter 3
Davidson, Richard. *The Emotional Life of Your Brain: How Its Unique Patterns Affect the Way You Think, Feel, and Live and How You Can Change Them*. New York: Hudson Street Press. 2012.

Porges, Stephen W. *The Polyvagal Theory: Neurophysiological Foundations of Emotions, Attachment, Communication, and Self-Regulation*. New York: W. W. Norton, 2011.

Siegel, Dan. *Mindsight: The New Science of Personal Transformation*. New York: Random House, 2010.

Siegel, Dan. *The Pocketguide to Interpersonal Neurobiology*. New York: Norton Press, 2012.

Chapter 5
Kabat Zinn, Jon. *Mindfulness Meditation in Everyday Life*. New York: BetterListen, 2014.

Chapter 6
Rafaeli, Eshkol. *Schema Therapy: Distinctive Features*. Hove, East Sussex: Routledge, 2010.

Rock, David. *Your Brain at Work*. New York: Harper Business Press, 2009.

Chapter 7
Byron, Katie. *Loving What Is*. New York: Three Rivers Press, 2003.

Childre, Doc Lew. *The HeartMath Solution*. New York: HarperOne, 2000.

Dupree, Ulrich. *Ho'oponopono: The Hawaiian Forgiveness Ritual as the Key to Your Life's Fulfillment*. Forres: Findhorn Press, 2012.

Feuerstein, George. *Tantra: Path of Ecstasy*. Boston, MA: Shambhala Press, 1998.

Mellin, Laurel. *Wired for Joy: A Revolutionary Method for Creating Happiness from Within*. Carlsbad, CA: Hay House, 2010.

Rosenberg, Marshall. *Nonviolent communication: A language of life*. Encinitas, CA: PuddleDancer Press, 2003.

Salzburg, Sharon. *Loving Kindness: The Revolutionary Art of Happiness*. Boston, MA: Shambhala Classics, 2002.

Siegel, Dan. *Mindsight: The New Science of Personal Transformation*. New York: Random House, 2010.

Chapter 8
Hanson, Rick. *Just One Thing: Developing a Buddha's Brain One Simple Practice at a Time*. Oakland, CA: New Harbinger, 2011.

CPSIA information can be obtained
at www.ICGtesting.com
Printed in the USA
LVOW12s0722160518
577229LV00025B/83/P